THIS LITTLE TOWN
OF
OTLEY

Harold Walker

THIS LITTLE TOWN
OF
OTLEY

*Memories, Reminiscences and Anecdotes
of the Metropolis of Wharfedale*

Harold Walker

R & S EDUCATIONAL SERVICES

1995

The publishers wish to point out that many of the
photographs in this book have been reproduced to
the highest standard possible, and due to their age,
may not be that to which present day readers
are accustomed.

I.S.B.N. 1 874724 16 4

First published 1974 by
Olicana Books Ltd.

This edition published 1995 by
R & S Educational Services
111 Ilkley Road
Otley
LS21 3JP

Printed and bound by
Smith Settle
Ilkley Road
Otley LS21 3JP

Contents

Foreword to the 1995 edition

I first met Harold Walker when, at the age of 83, he was considering compiling a book based on his collection of material and information on Otley and its environs. I was astonished to discover the extent of his collection — over 800 glass lantern slides, many articles he had contributed to the Airedale and Wharfedale Observer and the copious notes he had compiled in delivering innumerable lectures over 40 years. Editorial work on the book took over six months; that the book was an instant success on publication, and has maintained its appeal since, is testimony to the value of Harold Walker's work. Whilst there is much of historical value in the book it is not just a local history, for it is evident on every page that Harold Walker's lifelong interest in the history of his birthplace was matched by his affection for the town and its inhabitants. Many changes have taken place in recent years and the old merges with the new; companies, and industries, are no longer in existence; buildings demolished to make way for new, or modernised, or simply put to other uses — indeed, the premises in which this book is printed no longer operates as a textile mill, but provides opportunities for other businesses seeking accommodation. The town was also merged into Leeds Metropolitan District during "re-organisation" yet, despite all this, Otley retains its *essential* character which promotes the same affection among others as is displayed by Harold in this book. His reminiscences include many of the townspeople — notables, dignitaries and ordinary residents alike, who obviously felt the same about Otley and displayed this through their contributions to the life of the town. This book, in its own way, pays tribute to them for it is an irrefutable fact that what is *our* past was our forebears' present — as Coleridge wrote: *"the light which experience gives is a lantern on the stern, which shines only on the waves behind us"*. Up until the turn of the century Otley had not received much notice from historians and little had appeared in printed form about the town. When William Camden published his *Britannia* in 1586 and supervised its translation from Latin to English in 1610 he described Otley as: *"memorable for nothing but its situation under a huge craggy cliff called Chevin"*. The following pages will do much to dispel that view and confirm the special place that Otley holds in the hearts of many people, both here and overseas. This new edition of "A Little Town of Otley" will, I am sure, give a great deal of pleasure and interest to present and future readers who desire to discover more of their heritage and experience the attraction of *The Metropolis of Wharfedale*.

K. Smith

To the memory of my dear wife Lillian,
whose love and companionship over
fifty years of married life, gave me so
much happiness and contentment.

Foreword

I was born in the charming old Wharfedale market town of Otley in the year 1891, in a house near the Jubilee clock in the market place. My father, Charles Walker, a master printer, was in his time a noted local historian, who instilled into me a love for the town and district which I have never lost. For over 40 years I have lectured to many local organisations on the history of the town, showing some of the wonderful slides of "Old Otley" I have in my possession.

As I approached the age of eighty years, I thought it might be of interest to present and future generations if I wrote about some of the events that occurred, not only during my lifetime, especially in its early years, but also before I was born, which I had heard from others. I therefore commenced contributing articles to the local newspaper, "The Wharfedale and Airedale Observer", which have been favourably commented upon.

The basis of these articles, together with the script of some of my lectures, illustrated by many photographs and views, have been used in compiling this little volume.

Mrs. Hemans in one of her poems, wrote the following lines, which have always been associated in my mind with this little town of OTLEY — the place of my birth, and the home of my childhood so many years ago :

> "Teach them, your children, round the hearth,
> When evening fires burn clear,
> And in the fields of harvest mirth,
> And on the hills so dear,
> So shall each unforgotten word,
> When far those loved ones roam,
> Call back the hearts which once it stirred,
> To childhood's holy home."

HAROLD WALKER 1974

Acknowledgement

I would like to acknowledge the assistance and encouragement received from many sources during the preparation of this book, specifically mentioning the following:—

Ron D Biss and Sidney Smith, of the 'Wharfedale Observer' editorial staff, for their editorial work on my newspaper articles. Ken Smith, of the publishers, for his general advice on the design of the book and illustrations. Christine Dean for her typing of the manuscript. Paul Wood for his advice and encouragement. George, Gerald and Richard Aves for their photographic studies. Charles Ernest Mettrick, my godson, for his assistance as lanternist at my lectures.

My thanks to all.

HAROLD WALKER

Otley is an old market town which derives its name from Otho, a Saxon chieftain, whose possessions consisted of all the lands between the rivers Humber and Tyne, about the year A.D.620. In Doomsday it is called Othelai, and as a borough it is older than either Leeds or Bradford. The three castles on the Coat of Arms are those of Otley, Cawood and Wistow which belonged to the former Archbishops of York as "Lords of the Manor".

Jenny's cottage and rocks at summit

Chevin Hill

From Burras Lane

Standing like a sentinel guarding the town on the South, is lovely old Chevin, 925 feet above sea level, and to the North the hills rise majestically to the moors above.

The word "Chevin" is derived from the Celtic "Kefn", meaning a ridge, and from the top a wonderful view of the surrounding countryside can be obtained. Once it abounded in precipitous rock-work, and the general appearance was like the beautiful grandeur of Danefield. It has often been quoted in old Diaries, in which you read of the "ponderous crags of Chevin; of hardy travellers who had gained with thankfulness its dizzy heights". But in 1779, Chevin was enclosed, and now most of its rocks are hidden in tall plantations, or have been split and used for buildings. Blocks of stone were sent from Chevin to form the foundations of the Houses of Parliament.

I have always loved to wander round Chevin, where the air seems so pure, and life so remote, and on one such occasion this impelled me to write the following little memory :—

View of surrounding countryside from slopes of Chevin

1

The masher and his young lady

Reflections of an Erstwhile "Masher"

It was a natty, blue serge suit, the latest fashion, made to measure and all hand-sewn by Chippindales' the Tailors of Clapgate, Otley. The coat was double-breasted with high-cut lapels: the waistcoat buttoned nearly to the neck, and the trousers without permanent turnups, as these were not invented then. With two "fittings on" the price was two guineas!

A callow youth of seventeen in the year nineteen hundred and eight I was, nevertheless, in the parlance of the day, a "masher" and I felt it as, complete with buttoned boots, smart "billy-cock" hat, and walking stick, I sallied forth to give the natives a sight of my sartorial beauty.

After a walk into the town I decided to meander round the Chevin, and that's where fate stepped in for, at the summit, I passed two young ladies, strangers to me. A glance from one of them and, as so often happens, "my number was up". I don't know to this day whether or not the new suit had anything to do with my attracting her attention. But anyway, I'd "copped-on". Her home town was Yeadon — the "city on the hill" as we lowlanders used to call it — and so commenced a courtship nearly as long as Rachel's, followed by fifty years of happily-married life, until I lost her. God rest her soul!

Many years later I was doing the same walk, though not so spritely as of yore. Pausing near the spot where that electric glance had so changed the course of two lives, to soliloquise on the vagaries of existence, I happened to look down, and there I saw it — the stone — embedded in the soil, and nearly covered by the surrounding heather in full bloom. It bore a remote resemblance to an animal's head and face, and as it was in close proximity to the "cup and ring" stone nearby, in my passing fancy I wondered whether some Neolithic hand had been at work to embellish the last resting-place of a long-forgotten chieftain. But in any case thought I, not being so well versed in such matters, whether fashioned by hand, or a product of Mother Nature, it must have been there — a mute witness — when I first met my dear one: and so I picked it up

and "hugged" the whole fourteen pounds down to my house, where it now reposes in my garden giving me, oddly enough, a feeling of serenity. Sentimentality? Perhaps!

For in spite of what the younger generation think about we "crusty old floggers" there are not many of us who, for instance, when we see those pictures of newly-weds each week in the pages of the local newspaper, do not wish, in our hearts, good luck and a long, happily-married life to the smiling couples. I know I do.

So Stone Age or Mother Nature, what does it matter? Life goes on regardless for, as the late Albert Walker — the versatile "Whistling Commercial" — wrote many years ago:

"Yes, its grim old Chevin that saw us grow,
To manhood, then sees us all laid low;
Has seen the same for a thousand years —
The Valley's hopes, its joys, its tears."

A Former Public Beauty Spot

Near the quarries on the East Chevin Road is a large escarpment known as Pelstone Crag, on which are what appear to be prehistoric markings. The name is

Pelstone Crag

thought to be derived from the period when the district was peopled by a sheep-rearing tribe who would use the rocks for the drying and curing of the pelts of animals they had slaughtered for food. On the top of the Crag there are also carved the names of local people who have visited it during the past century or so. Up to 1914 the place was a popular venue for outings and picnics, and there were seats about on which to rest and view the surrounding countryside. At that time, a footpath led up to it from the road, reached by a stile in the wall near the top gate of Manby House, then the residence of Mr. Peter W. Musgrave. On the West side of Pelstone Crag was a small quarry, and whether or not this footpath was made in the first instance for the men who worked the stone there, the general public certainly acquired a right of way by virtue of the number of years they had been allowed to use it.

Mr. Peter W. Musgrave

An Old Boundary Stone

A short distance from Pelstone Crag, on the East Chevin road, near to its junction with Yorkgate, an interesting boundary stone was uncovered during repairs. Believed to date back to medieval times this stone, which probably marked the extent of the Manor and Liberty of Otley on the South side, bears the crude carving of the crossed keys which, together with the three castles of Otley, Cawood and Wistow (comprising the See of York) formed the Coat of Arms of the Archbishops when they were Lords of the Manor. It is worth noting that East Chevin Farmhouse nearby, formerly the Plough Inn before it became the Wilson's Arms during the last century, is also thought to have been at one time named the Cross Keys.

With the closing down of the quarry, Mr. Musgrave tried to stop the footpath by blocking the stile, but as fast as he did this, Mr. Joseph Bolton, Otley's rate collector at that time, removed the obstruction. Also two Otley residents — Mr. Fred Brockbank, a former headmaster of the National School, and Mr. Ernest Fieldhouse — for many years annually "walked" the path together on a Good Friday in order to keep it open for the public.

The old boundary stone

4

The river frozen

The River Wharfe

I often think that the main attraction of our town is the beautiful river which flows through it. Usually calm and tranquil the Wharfe, on occasion, can quickly become a raging torrent, hence its name "swift", from the Saxon word "Guerf". There is an old "saw" which reads :—

"Wharfe is clear, and Aire is lithe;
Where Aire kills one, Wharfe kills five."

In a severe winter it often freezes, providing good fun for the energetic.

The Nymph of the Wharfe is the Goddess Verbia, to whom it is supposed Claudius Fronto built an altar as a thanks-offering for an escape from drowning. In Myddleton Lodge, Ilkley, there is a beautifully worked stone which once formed part of it, according to what the Rev. B. J. Harker wrote in his "Rambles in Upper Wharfedale" published in 1869.

Winter on the river

The river Wharfe

The River in Flood

The bridge before Wharfemeadows Park

Otley's Ancient Bridge

Otley Bridge, which is of unique construction, spans the river at one of its widest parts — a distance of 140 feet. It is a good and substantial piece of masonry, dated about 1675, the previous bridge having been destroyed by flood. Actually it was built over two periods, the first portion being of ribbed and the second of dressed stone. In the "Leeds Intelligencer", dated 1774, there appeared an advertisement asking for estimates for the widening and repair of Otley Bridge, and this would be for the second portion, added in 1776. In October of the year 1775, to again quote the "Leeds Intelligencer": "There was a terrible storm of wind and rain, which lasted for 36 hours, and part of the bridge was thrown down". This would be just before its renovation the following year.

The bridge about 1900

7

The Parish Church

The Parish Church in 1903

The finest building in Otley is the Parish Church of All Saints. It is recorded by old historians that the first church was erected here by Edwin of Northumbria, after the bringing of Christianity to the North of England by Paulinus in A.D. 627.

The present edifice is Saxon, though it is safer to refer the North door to the Norman period. That the Chancel is Norman is evidenced by the round arch of the piscina, and the round-headed window on the North side was also of that period. For many years this window was blocked, but reopened when the Church was restored in 1851; at the time the Reverend Joshua Hart was Vicar. During further alterations in 1865-8, when the Vicar was the Reverend Samuel R. Anderson, an Organ Chamber and Vestry were built on the North side of the Chancel, and the Vicar's and Choir Vestries added on the South side.

Reverend Joshua Hart

Reverend Samuel R. Anderson

Fairfax tomb in the South Transept

The South transept was formerly called the "Denton Choir" in which is the splendidly carved memorial to Thomas, Lord Fairfax, and Helen Aske, his Lady, who was descended from the Cliffords of Skipton Castle. These were the grandparents of Sir Thomas Fairfax, friend of Oliver Cromwell who, with

Stone table at Farnley Hall

Sir Thomas, spent a day at Menston Old Hall, the home of Charles Fairfax, before the Battle of Marston Moor in 1644, when they held a consultation round a stone table in the garden. This table is now in the grounds of Farnley Hall. The silken standard used by the Roundheads at Marston Moor was, for many years, draped across the Fairfax tomb.

Ample evidence of the venerable age of the Church is to be seen in the fragments of early Saxon Runic Crosses, whose carvings have been fashioned by the most skilful craftsmen which that period, over 1300 years ago, could furnish. These fragments, which show traces of fire, were found built into the inner walls of the fabric during the restoration of 1865-8. A facsimile of one of them (the "Evangelist" cross) was erected in the churchyard, under the direction of the late Professor

Saxon Runic crosses

Collingwood, to the memory of the Otley men who died in the 1914-18 war, and is now in the Memorial Garden in Bondgate.

Perhaps the most interesting feature in the church tower is the clock, the works of which were all hand made in 1793 by George Goodall, of Aberford. The remarkable thing is that, although there are similar clock works up and down the country, these are the only known examples of this maker, who was really a watchmaker.

Details of the face of the clock will, perhaps, astonish most people. They are as follows, diameter of face 7 feet 4 inches; length of long hand to centre of clock face 3 feet 9½ inches. Total length of long hand 4 feet 8 inches. Length of short hand 2 feet 4½ inches. Width of each hand 10½ inches. Length of each figure 1 foot 3 inches. Diameter

The Church tower and clock

The clock works

of minute dot 2½ inches. The present dial and hands date from 1870, the previous ones having been given to Leathley Church.

For many years the Otley clock was looked after, repaired, and kept in good order by Mr. Joseph Nicholson, an Otley jeweller and watch repairer, and it was due to his unremitting care and attention that it always kept such good time. He and his father before him had charge of the church clock and mechanism continuously for more than 80 years, starting in 1871.

The Carillon and Parish Church Bells

In my young days as an apprentice in an old ramshackle building in Burras Lane, and despite the fact that I was being brought up in the Nonconformist faith, the Parish Church opposite was always of absorbing interest, and my father, who was steeped in the folklore of the town, often related to me something of its history.

Mr. Charles Walker

I was particularly taken with the Tower and the peal of bells, which I loved to hear, and the chiming of the carillon became part of my life over a period of ten years or so, hearing them, as I did, three or four times a day. These were installed during the Vicariate of the Rev. James Bailey, who was inducted in 1786 and died in 1816, when he was buried in Guiseley Parish Churchyard. The chimes were jocularly known as "Bailey's Fiddle", and were set to some of the popular tunes of that day. These included "There's nae luck about the house", "Paddy Whack", and "Yankee Doodle", amongst others. Eventually the mechanism went wrong as it seems to have done frequently at intervals over the years, and it was not put right until the year 1837, when the chimes were restored and new tunes were substituted such as "Home Sweet Home" and the "104th Psalm".

permission for the reproduction of an oil painting of the cleric, now in his possession.

In my early days there was a different tune for each day of the week, and this was played five times every four hours — at four, eight and twelve o'clock — changing at twelve midnight to a fresh tune. Those I remember are: Saturday "Home Sweet Home"; Sunday "O Worship the King"; Monday "Ye Mariners"; Tuesday "I love Jesus"; and Friday "The Last Rose of Summer". I cannot recall those for Wednesday and Thursday. "The Last Rose of Summer" was installed by Mr. Joseph Nicholson, father of Mr. Joseph Nicholson the watchmaker and jeweller. Unfortunately, the chimes are seldom heard nowadays.

Mr. W. M. Wilkinson

The Reverend James Bailey

The Rev. James Bailey was an ancestor of Mr. A. C. Walsh, of Guiseley, a well-known local historian and former bellringer, who is now the Secretary of Guiseley St. Oswald's Bellringers' Association. Mr. Walsh has kindly given

In addition to the carillon I loved to hear the church bells ringing, and indeed still do. Many years ago Mr. W. M. Wilkinson, a gardener and seedsman, who lived in a house and shop in Westgate, now demolished, wrote a poem about Otley which began :—

"This little town of Otley,
All other towns excels
In pleasant views and scenery,
And merry peals of bells."

11

With these sentiments I sincerely agree, particularly with regard to the last line, for in former days the fame of its bells and ringers was well known.

The peal of eight bells in the Parish Church belfry was hung in 1782 – to replace a peal of six bells hung in 1747 – and they were repaired in 1922. They have always been noted for their melodious tone, and there is a legend that the silvery note was obtained by a quantity of silver trinkets and coins having been thrown into the molten metal by a "galaxy of beauty and fashion" who visited the foundry when they were about to be cast. In the first-named year the cost was £389, and in the latter £900.

There was a crisis in 1888, when the sixth bell cracked right up to the waist. On examination it was found that the clapper had almost worn a hole through the bell. The remainder of the bells were also found to be so worn that the Churchwardens decided to have the cracked bell recast and the whole of the peal quarter-turned and re-hung with new fittings. The new bell weighed 12 cwt.

And if the bells were good, the men who rang them in the old days were dedicated to the art of campanology On February 20th 1787, a team of Otley ringers rang two whole peals of Holt's Triples in 6 hours 22 minutes, this being the first team to ever complete them in time and course in England. The list included some good old Otley names – Thomas Brown, James Kendall, Jonathan Cawood, John Horner, William Kendall, John Cawood, William Thompson and Benjamin Chippindale.

In 1882 another team of Otley ringers rang a "date touch" of Bob Major, consisting of 1882 changes, composed by Lister Cawood, who also conducted. The other participants were E. Cawood, Charlie Ralph, Fred Maston, James Horner, Charles E. Craven and William McGowan.

Bellringers for the Coronation Peal of Edward VII

In 1902 the Coronation Peal of King Edward and Queen Alexandra was rung by William Clough, Harry Nelson, James Horner, W. McGowan, Charlie Ralph, Fred Maston, Lister Cawood and F. Snowball. Mr. Clough was something of a "wag", and one of his sayings was "the devil in the church was either in the pulpit or the choir stalls".

During my long lifetime I have heard the bells peal on countless numbers of joyous occasions – and also, I remember, on sad ones. The tolling of the "minute" bell, on the death of a prominent citizen, was a regular custom. The tenor bell was tolled for an hour or two at one-minute intervals, then three other bells were sounded 6-8-10 times for a woman and 8-10-12 for a man, after which another bell rang out the number of years the deceased had lived. This practice has been discontinued for many years now, as also has the tolling of the "curfew" bell.

I wonder how many people know that the Ring O' Bells Inn, off Bondgate, got its name from the church bells. The first landlord of the inn, Mr. Jack Russell, was granted a beer licence about the beginning of this century for premises which had previously been a lodging house. Mr. Russell, taking a walk one Sunday evening when the bells were calling worshippers to Evensong, thought them so melodious that he decided "Ring O' Bells" should be the name of his new venture.

In days gone by the ropes used by the bellringers had to be stretched before they were attached to the bells, and this was done by suspending them from an iron bar sticking from the outside of the belfry tower, at a considerable height. A weight was then fastened to them and they were left for a period. On one occasion, when the Vicarage was in Church Lane, near the top of the Kirkgate Arcade, the then Vicar's wife happened to look out of one of the windows and was horrified to see her son sliding down a rope which was being stretched. The young rascal had climbed out of one of the windows in the Tower, on to the iron bar, to get to the rope. The sight made the poor lady swoon away.

An Interesting Churchyard

I was always, when young, particularly intrigued by the parties of visitors who, from time to time, came to look round the ancient church, and in those days there were considerable numbers, for it was noted as a place of historical and archaeological interest.

The Verger at this time was Mr. William Daphne, whose father, also named William, was the last Sexton and Licensed Clerk connected with the parish, having held that office for fifty years before his death in 1888, after which it was abolished. A gardener by profession, the latter had previously been in the employ of the Archbishop of York before coming to Otley, and remembered the effigy of the Archbishop being burned in York at the time of the passing of the first Reform Bill in 1839 when it was thought that the

primate had voted against it in the House of Lords. He was noted for his wit, and one anecdote he used to relate (according to my father) was about an old country parson who had come to preach in place of the Rev. S. R. Anderson, then the Vicar. This parson had put up at the White Horse Inn, and was caught in a shower of rain on his way to the service. In the vestry he said, "Just feel, Daphne, how wet I have got", to which that worthy replied, "Well, never mind sir, you'll be dry enough in the pulpit".

Mr. William Daphne, last licensed clerk and Sexton

The Parish Clerk whom Mr. Daphne succeeded was quite a different character altogether. Named Johnny Mountain, his standard of happiness was in the Woolpack Inn, where a special pint pot was kept for him known as "Johnny Mountain's Cuckoo Pot". Once, when on the spree, his wife was searching for him, and hearing he was at his favourite "house of call" she put her head inside the Tap Room door and shouted "Thou owt ta be ashamed o' thisen, thou lazy, drunken vagabond, spending thi' money here, when we havn't buried a wick soul for a fortnit". When Johnny was showing visitors round the church he would hurry them through, and then say "I'll tell ye what, they keep t'best ale at t'Woolpack, of onywhere in Otla".

However, to get back to the second Mr. William Daphne, the Verger, who showed visitors round the church in my time. After seeing the interior of the building, he always brought them into the churchyard to gather round gravestones of particular interest. At one of them I noted that after he finished speaking the members of the party always burst out laughing, and it was not for a considerable time, when I surrepticiously joined a group, that I found the reason for the hilarity.

This particular memorial stone was propped against the wall of the church (and is even now, all this time after, in the same place) and records the demise of Mary, wife of Ralph Arkley, and daughter of John Whitehead of Newall, who "Dyed" on October 5th 1749. Also Mary, whom she had with her former husband, William Dickinson, who "Dyed" in the first year of her age. "But", said

Mr. William Daphne, first Verger

Mr. Daphne, chuckling after reading this quaint epitaph, "it doesn't say what colour they were "dyed".

Links with John Wesley

Nearby in the churchyard a couple of tombstones mark the resting places of the Ritchie family, the great friends of the Rev. John Wesley, with whom the itinerant preacher used to stay on his frequent visits to Otley, and whose residence was in Kirkgate on the site of the present Arcade.

John Ritchie was a native of Edinburgh, and in the reigns of George II and George III he served in the Navy as a surgeon but, never partial to a seafaring life was always looking forward to retirement. He travelled throughout England looking for a pretty spot to settle in, and had the good taste to pick on the Otley district. He married a Miss

Tombstones of the Ritchie family

Robinson of Bramhope, and took up his final residence in the town. It was partly by his exertions that the building of the first Wesleyan Methodist Chapel in Otley — the old Drill Hall in Nelson Street, now demolished — where services, by law, could only be held out of Parish Church hours, was commenced in the year 1771. He died in 1780, and his funeral service was conducted in the Parish Church by the Rev. John Wesley, by consent of the Vicar at that time — The Rev. Henry Wilson.

Dr. Ritchie's grandson, Joseph, a doctor, in 1818, at the age of 27, answered the call of the British Government and led an expedition to North Africa, sponsored by the Colonial Office. After many privations the party eventually reached Murzuk, the capital of Fezzan, where the missionary-explorer contracted yellow fever and died after only a year's sojourn in the country. When leaving England he thought of home and wrote a poem which included the following touching lines :—

"And what if, far from thee my star must set,
Hast thou not hearts that will with sadness hear
The tale? And some fair cheek that will be wet?
And some bright eyes in which the swelling tear
Will start for him who sleeps in Afric's desert
drear."

In a graphic account of the expedition by Mr. W. F. Seals of Bramhope, published in "The Wharfedale Observer", he writes :— "So the mortal remains of an adventurous and learned son of Otley lie under the Saharan sands, far from that Otley churchyard which holds those of his forebears!"

Another interesting tombstone in the churchyard is that of Mr. William Snell, an early Wesleyan Methodist in Otley. He died in 1790 and I have heard that he also was buried by the Rev. John Wesley. If that is so, it must have taken place the year before the famous preacher himself died in 1791, at the age of 88.

Mr. Snell was steward to the Lord of the Manor. He lived at the Manor House, and was described as "witty and amusing beyond all description". He often sat up all night reading, visited all the gentry in the district, and was welcomed in every house. He took great pains to break through old and superstitious customs at Christmas and New Year, keeping out mummers and morris dancers, but to the horror of all Otley, gave "lights out" at nine o'clock, and let in Hannah Riley, a red-headed girl! A staunch "High-Church man", he tried hard to counteract the spread of Methodism, but, strange to relate, when the tremendous project was mooted of building a meeting-house in Otley, Mr. Snell gave his aid, became a trustee, and had his seat in the front gallery, where a six-mould candle burned before him at all the services.

For many years his tombstone bore a brass plate on it telling something of his character but made no mention of his eccentricities, such as keeping a black cat, black fowl, a black pig and a black cow, and of his having trained a goose to follow him. This brass plate was removed for renovation during the period Rev. T. J. Williams was Vicar, as it was in a bad state of disrepair.

As a footnote, may I say that I have never been able to discover who was the owner of the donkey supposed to be interred under the triangular stone near the church tower. Perhaps it is not the grave of a donkey at all but the resting place of the "old screw" that the Rev. John Wesley contended he was once sold in Otley. He wrote some slashing words to his followers in the town about them "doing as they would be done by" in the buying or selling of horses. "Write him down a knave who does not, and remember that a Methodist Knave is the worst of all Knaves!"

The Old Grammar School Building

The Grammar School

A building of pleasing architectural appearance is the Free Grammar School facing Manor Square, founded in the year 1611, and named Prince Henry's in compliment to the then Prince of Wales, who conferred the honour of a corporate body on the Trustees. The motto was "Deum Pave, Tomo Cave" — Fear God and Mind Thy Book — the last word of the motto being a pun on the name of the founder, a man named Thomas Cave, of Wakefield. He had been a travelling sales or packman in the district for many years and amassed a moderate fortune, some of which he desired to leave to benefit the children of the people amongst whom he had traded. He was known as a "copman", and the name is perpetuated in Upper Copmanroyd, the right-of-way running from Carr Bank Road just below the Roebuck Inn (or "Spite") across the fields to Farnley Lane near Mount Pleasant Farm. Lower Copmanroyd formerly ran past Old Newall Hall, and was obliterated when the Newall Housing Estate was constructed in 1928.

At one time Thomas, Lord Fairfax, the Parliamentary general, was one of the Trustees, and amongst the former Head-masters were the Rev. James Bailey and the Rev. Joshua Hart.

The first school built was a one-storied building with a door in the centre. A stone over the doorway bore the words "Founded by Gift". This build-ing was pulled down and the present one built from the old materials. It was opened in 1840, but owing to the limited endowment, finally closed in 1874. In 1813 the Court and Sessions of his Grace, the Archbishop of York, Lord of this Liberty were held in the School. The lower rooms were also, for many years, used as a Courthouse for civil and criminal cases, before the present build-ing in Courthouse Street was erected. Mr. Matthew Whitaker Thompson, of Parkgate, Guiseley was, on one occasion, a witness in a case held before a particu-larly pompous judge. "And what, may I ask, is your occupation?" asked the Judge loftily. "Well, sir," replied Mr. Thompson, quietly, "When I am in Bradford I am a Brewer; when in London, a Barrister; and when at home in Guiseley, I am a gentleman!"

A relic of the Archiepiscopal Quarter

16

Sessions held in the old Grammar School for many years is Gallows Hill, just below the Cemetery in Pool Road, where felons condemned by the Justices were hanged.

Old Gallows Hill

In 1297 Ralph Brum was executed there for robbery, and his lands, said to be worth 24s.4d., and chattels worth 14/- were forfeited, according to the old Parish Register. In a later century Thomas Teasdaille was hanged for stealing goods to the value of 3s.9d. from the Prioress of Esholt. It was also the custom, until 1150, to drown women thieves, and in those days a branch of the river Wharfe washed the sides of Gallows Hill. The last person hanged there was John Conyers, a bellman, on June 12th 1614.

The premises were eventually sold to Mr. Thomas Constable for £800. They were recently acquired by the Sam Chippindale Foundation — a charitable trust instituted by the Otley-born man who has had such a successful career as a town developer.

A Georgian Dwelling

The Manor House is a residence looking on to the centre of the town. It is a Georgian building, supposed to have been designed by Mr. Carr, the York Architect. When built by Mr. Wilson, Steward to the Lord of the Manor, over 200 years ago, it was intended to have it further up the river on the site of the old Episcopal Palace. The lawyer's wife, however, wished it built where she could see up Kirkgate, and on Mr. Wilson being called away on business for some time, she had the pegs removed, the foundations dug on the present site, and the building proceeding by the time he got back. As the Rev. Joshua Hart wittily remarked in one of his lectures; "If man was head, woman was neck, and could twist the head which way she liked". It was formerly occupied by Mr. Thomas Constable who was descended from the Earls of Nithsdale. He was instrumental in bringing over to Otley 100 families from Ireland, during the time of the Potato Famine about 1847. He was also the prime mover in the building of the Roman Catholic Church in Otley, a beautiful edifice dedicated to the Blessed Virgin Mary and All Saints, and he and his sister defrayed almost the whole cost — £4,000.

The Manor House

17

The Old Hall

One of the most interesting pieces of architecture in the town, I have always thought, is the Old Hall, situated in Kirkgate, opposite the Jubilee Clock. An early Georgian residence erected about 1704, it was converted into two shops in 1840. The building is of three storeys and five bays, with a one-bay pediment, all surrounded by a stone balustrade. In recent years this pediment was demolished, and superseded by the present wooden structure. When the building was first made into shops the stone pillars of the porch were purchased by Dr. Thomas Shaw, and placed in front of the residence he had erected in Boroughgate, now the offices of public authorities. It was at one time the abode of Mr. Thomas Lacon Barker, who died in 1773. He laid the foundation of the

Doorway taken from the Old Hall

family of Viscount Halifax through his daughter Caroline marrying, in 1770, Captain Charles Wood, of Bolling Hall, Bradford, an eminent Naval Officer who died of wounds received when, as commanding officer of His Majesty's ship "Worcester", he was in action with the French Fleet in the East Indies, in September 1782.

It used to be said that in the bay of the window of the pediment the outline of an old man sitting on a chair and looking towards Chevin had been seen on several occasions by occupants of the house. My brother Jimmy's wife Kathleen, daughter of Mr. Fred Suttle, was born and lived there for over 20 years, and I once asked her if there was any truth in the story. She said, however, that although none of their family had ever seen the old man, several times a chair, which usually stood in another part of the room, had been found in the bay, although nobody ever remembered moving it there!

The Old Hall

Old Corner Shop

The old Corner Shop about 1890

One of the most impressive buildings I remember in my early days was "The Old Corner Shop" near the Jubilee Clock at the junction of Kirkgate and Market Place, in which J. W. Hellewell carried on the business of grocer and provision merchant, and sold confectionery made on the premises. Now the store of a multiple firm of pharmacists, it also dates back to early Georgian days, and at one time was one of the tallest and most imposing business premises in the town, dominating the centre, being then a storey higher than it is at present. Previously it was, for a number of years, owned by three brothers – John, Charles and Fred Walker – who resided at Grove House, a big Georgian residence in Bondgate demolished to make the Memorial Garden and part of Crossgate – the road which took the place of Sugar Street. Grove House was, towards the end of the eighteenth century, in the occupation of a clergyman known locally as Parson Wilson, who was not connected with Otley Parish Church, but was Curate -in-Charge of the Parish of Weston. Of independent means he was, by all accounts, a "sporting personality", and kept stables and kennels on the opposite side of Bondgate, where the Bus garage and offices now stand.

According to Parson Wilson, the hares of that day were not up to hiding where a hunting clergyman could not start them. "The hares are fools", said a drab Quaker to the sporting parson, "were I a hare thee should'st never find me". "Ah, where is that Neighbour Broadrib, for I know every place from Whin Cover to the Sand Pit?" "I would hide in thy study, Friend Tally-ho, and lie in form beside thy big Bible".

The "Bowling Green" Hotel in Bondgate was built in 1757 as the Assembly Rooms where the gentry met regularly, and the country dance and "pas-de-seul" went on to the sound of harp and violin. A theatre was also in a part of the building, and in one company, a merry, buxom girl – Harriet Mellon – often appeared with the actor, Edmund Kean, before he achieved fame in London.

On one occasion, after appearing at Otley, Harriet was walking over Stainburn Moor to join the Company at Harrogate when she was caught in a storm, and was soon drenched with rain. Luckily however, the owner of the "Corner Shop" overtook her on his horse, and although she was saturated with rain, her shawl a sop and her bonnet a pulp, took her up behind him. In after years, when she had become a famous actress, the wife of the London Banker, Coutts, and eventually the Duchess of St. Albans, in her ducal dignity she never forgot the kindness of the Otley people, and always bought her hams at The Old Corner Shop.

I was born in the building – now a butcher's shop – in Market Place, next door to the Old Corner Shop, in 1891, a few years after Mr. J. W. Hellewell came to the town, and his son Arthur was one of my teachers when I was a scholar at the Wesleyan Sunday School. One of the chief recollections of my boyhood days is of the succulent buns Hellewell's made for distribution to the Sunday School scholars after the annual Whitsuntide "sing" in the Market Place. Two buns and an orange in a bag to each scholar – they were lovely!

The Mechanics' Institute

The Otley Civic Centre was formerly known as the Mechanics' Institute, and the centenary of its opening was celebrated in 1971. For the major part of that period it was the academic, cultural and social centre of the community. The name was changed after the building had been modernised and redecorated by Otley Council, in accordance with plans for the redevelopment of the Otley town centre.

Mr. William Ackroyd

The real roots of the Institute were a Useful Instruction Society, which had its beginnings in a cottage in Victoria Yard, off Kirkgate, in 1807, and transferred to the Salem Schoolroom in Bridge Street, after having amalgamated

Mechanics Institute, about 1900

20

with the Mutual Instruction Society that was held there.

Mr. William Ackroyd, founder of the worsted spinning mills in Ilkley Road, was the first President of this, and the membership cards were printed from a woodcut representing the arts and crafts; also it showed the Otley Coat of Arms, and the motto of the old Prince Henry's Grammar School, which at that time was closed down. Mr Jabez Horner was the first secretary, and as he

The first membership card

was also a wood carver, it is thought that he designed and made the wood-cut, as his initials were at the bottom.

From these beginnings sprang one of the Mechanics' Institutes then becoming so popular up and down the country. The first premises were the old Wesleyan Chapel in Nelson Street (afterwards the Drill Hall), and the building was altered to provide a reading room, several classrooms, and a library, with a large hall over the lot on the second storey.

The first curator and librarian was

Mr. James Brown, a postman, who held the position for 26 years. At that time there was no weekly newspaper in the town, so each Christmas Mr. Brown issued his own broadsheets in which the main events of the past twelve months, published in rhyme, were recorded.

In those days very few people could read or write and the centre became popular. In 1851, for instance, it is recorded that gratuitous instruction in reading, writing, arithmetic, grammar and geography, were given by Dr. Kerr, a private school master, Rev. J. S. Hastie, Salem Minister, and Mr. Price, headmaster of the National School.

In addition to classes, there were entertainments, concerts and "penny readings". Some interesting lectures were also given. One, by the Vicar of Otley, the Rev. Joshua Hart, entitled "Our Valley", in 1865, commenced at the source of the River Wharfe, taking in all the villages on its banks from Outhershaw, until it found the Ouse at Nun Appleton, to mix with the Humber, after running more than 60 miles.

After some years of steady progress in Nelson Street, it was found that those premises were too small, and so the first portion of the present structure in Cross Green, built on the site of some old

Thatched cottages in Cross Green, site of the Mechanics Institute

21

Building in progress

A couple of weeks before the advertised time of the official opening a disastrous storm visited the valley, and the Maypole was struck by lightning, which also demolished the old Market Cross from which butter and other dairy commodities used to be sold when the market was held near the village green and Maypole — before the present Butter Cross and Market Place were constructed. Piles of stones from the Cross, some of them weighing half a ton, were deposited around the Maypole, and the new Mechanics Institute was so bombarded by flying stones that all the front windows were broken and the outside wall so damaged that the opening ceremony had to be put off. Stones, indeed, were found on the roof.

thatched cottages, and facing the Maypole and the village green, was commenced. The foundation stone was laid on June 19th, 1869, by Mrs. C. H. Dawson of Weston Hall, assisted by her son, Master W. C. Dawson. The cost was £4,000 and the building was opened on October 31st, 1871, free of debt, with a soiree and public meeting.

Over the years the large hall of the Institute has played a big part in catering for the social life of the community, and many local people must have nostalgic memories of happy times spent there. Balls, dances, concerts, bazaars and functions of every description have been held, including the travelling theatrical companies who used to produce old melodramas and plays like "Convict 99", "The Face at the Window" and "Maria Martin".

The Art School wing was added in 1895, mainly through the efforts of Mr. Alfred Marshall, who persuaded Mr. John Yeadon, trustee of the Craven estate at Bramhope, to allocate the sum of £700 from funds left for educational purposes, towards the object.

Together with an amount of £1,467, from a successful bazaar known as "The Model Village" organised by Mr. Henry Dacre, this was sufficient for the extension to be completed, after the foundation stone had been laid by Mrs. Ayscough Fawkes, of Farnley Hall.

The Maypole struck by lightning

When Prince Henry's Grammar School was revived in 1918, the Institute rooms were used until the new school in Farnley Lane was built.

Laying the foundation stone of the Art School

Like many other things, with changing times the Mechanics' Institute fell on evil days, and as the Directors could not "carry on" financially, they handed over the building to the Urban District Council.

The "Beehive" Store

Before he left Otley many years ago to reside in Cornwall, Mr. Walter Moss, an old friend of mine, was well-known to many people as a prominent tradesman in Otley, and Chairman of the local Chamber of Trade. After the death, about 1940, of his father, he became manager of the family business of W. B. Moss and Sons, Grocers and Provision Merchants, and guided it through the difficult war period of food rationing. The firm went out of business eventually and the building it occupied in Market Place is now the self-service shop of a multiple store. Before the present structure, which extends from the Market Place to Kirkgate, was erected, the site was occupied by a grocery shop known as the "Beehive", and several other shops, run respectively by a greengrocer, a barber (afterwards a sweet shop) and premises which were in turn occupied by a toy dealer, a milliner and the late Mr. George Harrison when he transferred his newsagents' business there from Market Street.

W. B. Moss and Sons

The old "Beehive" at one period belonged to a man named Ned Mawson and a story is told that he once asked Ike Pollard, the old billposter and bellman, if he would like to earn a shilling. Of course Ike said he would. "Has tha got a gun?" asked Mawson. "Tha'll want a gun as ah want thee to shoit summat". So Ike borrowed a gun from Dick Thompson, the landlord of the Bluebell Inn in Manor Square — a public house made redundant many years ago. "Is it loaded?" queried Mawson, and on being assured that was the case said, "Tha sees t'Beehive, well ah want thee to shoit t'monkey there is on top of it". "Ah can't see ony monkey," replied Ike, as he gazed at the building. "But there is," persisted Ned, "a gert big one sitting reight across t'top wi' its feet touching both sides, and it will be well worth a shilling if tha' can topple it over."

Needless to say Pollard did not earn that shilling, for the monkey was, of course, the mortgage on the building. But shortly afterwards Mr. Stephen Parkinson shot it down with golden bullets by purchasing the business, and he created a highly successful concern before selling out to Moss and Sons, whose original business was at Hitchin, Herts.

The Beehive store in 1890

Where is Klondyke?

Klondyke after a flood

"Klondyke" was the name locally given to the piece of land near the river on which the Bridge Avenue and Farnley Lane houses were built. The field, as it was then, belonged to Dr. Williamson, a medical practitioner who lived and had his surgery at "Romagna House" in Boroughgate, demolished a good few years ago, the site of which is now part of the premises of a firm of car dealers. Dr. Williamson also owned all the land adjacent to the river from the Bridge to the Damstones and down this ran a foot-path from the Bridge end to Farnley Lane. When he decided to sell the field for building purposes, buyers were invited to "stake their claims", and as this was about the time of the second "gold rush" in Alaska, near the Yukon River, in 1898, the place became known as "Klondyke".

Actually, the name arose from an association of ideas, for one of the first purchasers of plots was Mrs. Joseph Pickles, mother of Mr. Thomas Pickles who had the boating rights on the river for many years. Mrs. Pickles had been left a legacy by an uncle in Australia, who had made his money by gold mining in Ballarat, and this fact, together with the "staking of claims", as was done in the Yukon, prompted the name.

Another factor which may have influenced the name is that an Otley man took part in the "Gold Rush" to the Klondyke about this time. He was Thomas, son of Mr. Thomas E. Buck, for 40 years a bank manager in Otley, and also the first treasurer to the Otley Local Board of Health (the forerunner of the Urban District Council) when it was formed in 1864.

The younger Thomas received his education at Dr. Kerr's Collegiate School in Burras Lane (now the Musgrave Memorial Hall), chose a sea-faring career, and learned his profession on one of the last of the old sailing ships. He was a colourful character and adventured all over the world before leading an expedition of 22 persons to the Klondyke in 1898 in a search for gold, and also to trade along the Yukon river in their steamer "Research". The party was navigating the river for only the first time, however, when it was struck by illness which resulted in the death of their leader.

Dr. Williamson built and resided in the last house in Bridge Avenue nearest to Farnley Lane, which has been converted into two flats by the Council, who now own it. Between it and the river was a small enclosure where the Doctor ran his horses. Early in the 1920's Otley Council, who had bought the land for the laying out of Wharfemeadows Park, constructed the open-air swimming pool on a portion of it.

It was on "Klondyke" by the way, that the old Otley Salem Cricket Club played its matches and it was also used by the Otley Clarence Association Football Club about 1898.

Thomas Buck on right

The Old Market

Otley Market in 1898

Otley Market is known to have been uniformly attended and maintained for over 700 years. It was in 1222 that King Henry III created Otley Feast by licensing Fairs in the town on the old vigil and day of the Feast of St. Mary Magdalene — July 21st and 22nd — and also authorised weekly markets on Mondays and Fridays. In 1872 the Ecclesiastical Commissioners, as Lords of the Manor, transferred their rights to the tolls in the market place and streets of

26

Otley on the Feast and Fairs, for the sum of 5/- per annum (afterwards extinguished by payment of £4.10s). Over a century and a half ago the cattle markets were held in Cross Green. They were then removed to Manor Square, which at that time was known as the Cattle Market, where the old brick and timber Shambles stood up to 1872. The first fortnightly Fairs, established in 1866, had as many as 400 beasts and 1300 sheep brought together on the Friday Fair days. The cattle were finally removed to the Licks, where Pens had been erected, in 1876.

The market square and the centre of the town have always been occupied by the stalls of market traders and in my young days these were mostly Otley shopkeepers — several of them butchers — and farmers' wives from the outlying districts. The latter used the seats of the Butter Cross for displaying their dairy produce — rabbits, chickens, ducks, eggs, butter, etc. Eggs were sold at so many for a shilling, and butter was in rolls of 24 ounces or half rolls. Traders in live stock — puppies, pet rabbits, guinea pigs, etc., hens and ducks — also used the Butter Cross. One such family I remember in this line were the Howgate's from Yeadon, who came for many years. You may perhaps have heard the story of the old farmer woman who used to sit in the Butter Cross at times with a big basket full of eggs for sale. Asked one day if they were all fresh, she replied "Aye, all on 'em; I've nobbut three hens an' they've laid t'lot!"

The Shambles, demolished in 1872

The Licks cattle market in 1884

The market square

Market Personalities of the Past

I don't know whether or not it was because I was born in a house near the Jubilee Clock, but I have always been fascinated by the Friday Market, and the various characters who attended. I well remember such wags as "Pot Bob" Morrison from Knaresborough, who could juggle with half a dozen dinner plates better than many a music hall artiste, and whose quick repartee always kept the crowds amused; Harry Sharp, the "Oilcloth King", from Bradford; and "Cudball" Cooper, the cattle "doctor" from Yeadon. There were vendors of patent medicines that were claimed to cure all ills, from corns to stones in the kidney, and whose rheumatism pills, if taken regularly, would land sufferers half way up the

The market in Kirkgate

centre of Chevin, before they even knew they had started; also "Eye Lickers" who, for free, licked incipient cataracts from the eyes of anyone so afflicted, were frequent visitors and always drew a crowd of sightseers. One Indian gent who specialised in this type of cure, I remember, took cararacts from the eyes of a young man I knew, enabling him to join the Army in the first world war. Another chap folks enjoyed listening to was a character with long hair and a pointed beard, like Buffalo Bill. He sold hair restorer guaranteed to "grow whiskers on a bladder of lard", and nobody suspected that he wore a wig himself and was as bald as a coot! The most macabre display of all, however, was made by a man who pulled out teeth at a tanner a time. There were no such things as anaesthetics in teeth extraction in those days; the teeth were just yanked out with a pair of pliers, and the poor patient's howls as he submitted to the torture simply delighted the crowd — they just loved it! Many years ago we had a Druggist in Otley who also pulled out teeth without an anaesthetic. Named Albert A. Benn, he occupied one of the shops in Boroughgate, opposite the Maypole, and his fee, I remember, was also sixpence a tooth. Medical men did the job as part of their duties, and Dr. Galloway once took out one for me when I was a lad — and I believe he even enjoyed doing so. A Druggist named Mr. Moore, with a shop in High Street Yeadon used to extract teeth and store them in big bottles which he exhibited in his shop window, bearing labels stating "Weary Molars now at Rest!" Whenever I was passing I always stopped to gape at them — one of the sights of Yeadon in the "Good old days".

Mr. James Tempest, who founded a butchering business in Boroughgate well over a hundred years ago, had a stall in Kirkgate near the top of Boroughgate, where he was assisted by his son, also named James. Mr. Wood of New Market, father of Mr. Herbert Wood — for many years secretary of the Wharfedale Auc-

Tempest's butcher stall

tion Mart Ltd. — had one near the Jubilee Clock in the Market Square; and Mr. Brown, whose premises were in Westgate stood outside the "Blue Bell" Inn in Manor Square. The pub building is now a Bank.

Mr. Wood's stall

Brown's stall, Manor Square

Mr. Middlemass, an Askwith farmer and butcher, had a meat stall outside Moss's store in the Market Place and sold unskinned rabbits at 6d. each. One character I remember frequenting the market was Mr. William Thompson, a stout old gentleman who was known as Otley's "John Bull". A retired butcher, whose house and shop next to the "Cross Pipes" Hotel in Westgate are now pulled down, he spent a lot of time sitting in his doorway — "a tight fit"! On one such occasion a young chap passing by accosted him. "I say maister" said he, "may I ask ye a question?" "Why of course lad," replied Mr. Thomp-

R.R. Thompson, Otley's "John Bull"

son. "What is it?" "Well, do ye ever have t'stummick ache?" "Of course I do t'same as other folk." 'My' returned the lad as he scuttled away, "it will be a big ache Maister — a big ache!"

The Saturday market at the turn of the century was not as big as it is to-day — just a few stalls then near the Jubilee Clock selling sweets, and fruit and vegetables, etc. — but it did not close at 4 p.m. as now. Shops were all open until a comparatively late hour and the town was very busy. Butchers' shops, in particular, were always crowded round about 10 p.m., for the meat had to be sold, there being no refrigerating methods, and it would not keep over the week-end. Therefore joints were very cheap, and good Sunday dinners ensured. Refrigerators meant the end of cheap meat for working-class families.

Saturday nights in the summer months were always lively in Otley, for the local Band invariably gave concerts in Manor Square, and there was always a ring for the dancers to enjoy themselves — the going was rough, but the pleasure real!

The Recreation Hall

About the beginning of the present century, the centre of social life in Otley was the Recreation Hall in Church Lane, where many people spent some of the happiest hours of their lives within its comfortable precincts. Founded by Mr. Henry Dacre, an Otley solicitor with offices in the Old Grammar School building in Manor Square, the plans were prepared by Mr. Alfred Marshall, and the Foundation stone laid in 1895 by Mr. Ayscough Fawkes, of Farnley Hall. The building was undertaken by Messrs. T. and W. Maston, and when completed it had a bright interior, and the Concert Hall was panelled in oak taken from the Salem Chapel, then being rebuilt. In 1897 this was named the "Queen's Hall", in commemoration of Queen Victoria's Daimond Jubilee. It was decorated and furnished in the style of a winter garden, with a stage at one end, galleries on three sides, and a maple floor. Used for concerts, lectures, Sunday services, dramatic performances, social evenings, roller skating and dances, etc., it fulfilled a long-felt want, and for many years was very popular, being open every day, except Sundays. There were also a reading room, smoke room, club rooms, a dark room fitted for photographers, and an arcade running the whole length of the main building which could be used as a supper room. A bathroom fitted with slipper and a plunge bath merited a charge of 4d. from members, and 6d. from non-members. The grounds were laid out as a Japanese Garden, with rustic seats and summer houses, a fountain and flower beds, and periodical concerts and alfresco

Japanese Gardens

31

The Recreation Hall

Queen's Hall

entertainments were given in the summer months. The charge for admission to the gardens for non-members was 2d. The motto adopted was "Prospice non Respice" – Forward not Backward – and for many years this principle was adhered to.

Mr. Dacre built a large house named "Hawthornden" in Bradford Road, Otley, and the Brass Band raised at the Recreation Hall was named after it.

Founded in 1891, this Band played in London and the Isle of Mann, on occasion, and became very much sought after in the district for outside events. Over the years he put on many musical plays and concerts in the Queen's Hall For a long time he was organist and choirmaster at the Otley Congregational Church.

One of his musical associates was Mrs. S. E. Watkinson, a talented pianist

Caley Hall

and a member of his inside orchestra, who was also a teacher of music. Mrs. Watkinson composed a piece of music in honour of the Hawthornden Band, which she named the "Hawthornden Waltz". It became very popular, and was often played at dances in the district. I have waltzed to its lilting tune many times in my young days.

In his later years Mr. Dacre went to reside at Caley Hall, near Pool, where he died. For some time after his death concert parties and plays by local amateurs kept the Recreation Hall going, but as these ceased to be patronized, the grounds became a scrap yard, and the building a warehouse. Eventually the latter came into the possession of the local Council, and was demolished some time ago.

The Caley Hall estate eventually came into the possession of the late Mr. William Whiteley of the Pool Paper Mills firm, and when he eventually had the place pulled down, a portion of it was erected at the side of the Old Grammar School building in Manor Square, Otley.

Caley Hall was once the Hunting Lodge of the Gascoignes and their arms, together with initials and the date of 1582 were on one of the old box pews taken out of Otley Parish Church at the restoration in 1865-9. From the Gascoignes the estate passed to the Daltons, and then to the Atkinsons, the last of whom married a Miss Fawkes, of Farnley, whose son sold the estate to Mr. W. Fawkes, of Farnley Hall, his relation. The park was made in 1820, and ten years later was well-stocked with red and fallow deer, according to Dr. Thomas Shaw's "History of Wharfdale" published in 1830. There were also zebras, goats and wild hogs, all of which were fed in Winter with beans, turnips and hay. Axis, or deer of the Ganges, the most beautiful of the deer tribe, were also reared. The name "Deer Park" survives to this day, the high rocks in it being known as Caley Crags. It is now part of Otley Danefield Estate.

Interior of the Hall

Drill Hall Memories

Watching the tearing down of the old Drill Hall in Nelson Street was, to me, like attending a requiem, for so many episodes in my life have been connected with it.

The Drill Hall in Nelson Street

My first association with the building, originally erected in 1772 as the first meeting house of the Otley Wesleyan Methodist community, was in 1907. In that year the late Viscount Haldane, Minister for War, reorganised our Volunteer Army by introducing a Volunteer Territorial Force equipped on the lines of the regulars, but for home defence only. Rumours were flying around Otley that the local Royal Engineers Volunteers Company was to be disbanded and a "Flying Column" — whatever that might be — of the Army Service Corps (disrespectfully referred to by other branches of the Army as "Ally Sloper's Cavalry") was to be established in its place.

At that time I was 16 years of age, and apprenticed to my father, a local printer with a small business, and worked from 6.30 a.m. to 6 p.m. daily, except Saturdays, when I finished at 12 noon. My pocket money had just been increased from 6d. per week to two shillings, and although I could make another 4d. or 6d. per week by selling a batch of spoiled copies of a weekly advertising sheet called "The Wharfedale Times" published by my father, to Mr. Light who kept a fried fish and chip shop in New Market, my means were still pitifully low.

There was plenty going on in the old town in those days for which cash was necessary — several dances a year; the Recreation Hall, with its many attractions, the swimming club which used the river near the north side of the bridge for its activities; and the Rugby Football Club that was being revived at that time which used the field near Manor Street (now an open space for the use of the town's inhabitants) before the present rugby ground in Cross Green was acquired. Also the Agricultural Show, the Friendly Societies' Demonstration and Gala, the Foal Show, and the Chrysanthemum Show. Many good concerts were given by local societies; and there were high-class lectures by speakers nationally famous; also occasional visits by travelling theatrical companies who put on quite good plays and melodramas. No Picture Houses, except the cinematograph shows at Otley Feast in August and the November Statute Hirings, when the travelling variety in large tents in which one sat on wooden benches were erected in the fairground in the Licks. The admission charge was 2d., and the pictures flickered and "rained" through half-hour programmes.

Anyway, the new Territorial Army took my fancy, and when I found that by enlisting into the moribund Engineers Volunteers before the end of the year I could transfer to the new force on a year-to-year engagement instead of four years, I "took the shilling", giving my

34

Friendly Society's demonstration and gala

age as 17. This privilege was taken advantage of by almost all the Royal Engineers Volunteers, those with ranks retaining them.

Early in 1908 we were absorbed into the new Territorial Army, and found that we were a Royal Artillery Unit – the 10th (Otley) Battery, 4th West Riding Howitzer Brigade, equipped with five-inch horse-drawn guns, and commanded by Col. W. Stopham Dawson, of Ashfield House. The new adjutant was a Regular Army officer – Capt.

Recreation Hall entry at a demonstration

*N.C.O's of the Otley Company of the Engineers
Volunteers in 1906*

The Volunteers marching to the station bound for Chatham camp, 1912.

Muirhead, R.F.A. — and the permanent staff instructor was Sgt. (afterwards Sgt. Major) Tom Seymour, also a Regular, who had seen service in the Boer War and afterwards in India.

The Drill Hall had been purchased

Five inch horse-drawn Howitzers

by Mrs. Emma Dawson, of Weston Hall, at the time her eldest son, Col. William Christopher Dawson, was Captain in charge of the Otley Company of the Royal Engineers Volunteers, but it was later sold to the Yorkshire Territorial Army Association, who had the gun shed built in the large yard adjoining.

Things very soon got moving. We were issued with khaki uniforms — riding breeches with a thin red stripe down the side seams, service jackets, cavalry great coats with full skirts, peaked caps and cap badges, army boots, overalls and, most impressive of all to me, big clanking spurs.

How I enjoyed the first church parade that year when, headed by the Brigade Band under its conductor, Bandmaster T. P. Newton, we marched to the Parish Church where the Vicar, the Rev. R. Pattinson, preached a rousing sermon and we lustily sang "Fight the Good Fight".

My father of course by this time knew I had joined the Battery, as he caught me one evening coming out of the Drill Hall smoking a big pipe (tobacco was only 4d. an ounce in those days) but he had to make the best of the matter.

Training went on apace that year. I had been picked out to be a signaller and was being instructed in semaphore, with two flags. To get us somewhat prepared for the first Divisional Camp in August was a herculean task. Riding school was on two evenings a week in the Bridge Field (where the Cattle Auction Mart now is) on big dray horses owned by Messrs. Pepper, the railway goods carriers. Constant repetition by the riding instructor of the old gag, "Who told you to dismount?" when we fell off a nag soon ceased to be funny, and sore behinds and knees were more than common.

The first annual camp of the 49th Division was held at Redcar for two weeks. My father would let me off for only one of these weeks, and so I went on the second one. The late J. B. Dawson, I remember, travelled with me. We were the only ones in the Battery who did not go for the full fortnight, and the brown faces after a week's sunshine and sea air, of those who did, were in sharp contrast to our white ones.

Issued with three blankets and a palliasse which I filled with straw at the wagon lines, I was allocated a place in a bell tent. Afterwards out to see the sights of Redcar in the evening with my two pals — Dalby Russell and Wilkes Harrison. What decorations there were in the town! Huge streamers across the streets carried slogans like "Welcome Terriers, our Defenders" and flags and bunting were flying almost everywhere. Of course I had to buy myself a riding switch with our regimental crest on the handle.

Tired but happy, I returned to camp to find that some "so-and-so" had pinched my blankets and I had to spend the rest of the week sleeping in my trousers with my great coat over me for warmth. As the blankets were back in my place at the end of the camp ready for me to hand in, I considered myself lucky not to have had to pay for them out of the shilling a day which was my army pay for the week. How naive I was in those dim and distant days.

Over the years I can still remember the gallops across the sands to Marske, on one of which Walter Atkinson lost his cap; also my first night-picket duty from 11 p.m. to 2 a.m. — three hours of misery — when half the nags in the lines, said to have been lent by Mr. Albert Mills, a Guiseley Farmer, at £5 per head for the duration of the camp, broke loose. Possessed of devils, they careered about amongst the other horses and I was scared stiff. As soon as one was hobbled another broke away and they were kicking and tossing all over the place.

The parting of the ways between the Battery and I came unexpectedly the following year, just before I was intending "signing on" for a further period. I had "copped on" by this time and was walking out with a young lady from Yeadon — "the city on the hill" as we used to call it. On Chevin, one Sunday, we passed a couple of the Battery N.C.O.'s — Sgts. Joe Spence and Alf Wilkinson — who probably wished

to assert their authority (this was in the good old days when England was supposed to be the land of the free). "Don't thee forget," said one, "There's a drill on Tuesday neet". "Aye," said t'other, "Tha'll be for it if tha misses".

We walked on for a while in silence, my young lady and I. Then it came. "Do you allow people to speak to you like that?" she said. "I'm sure I wouldn't!" So my uniform went in (including the clanking spurs) — not without a tinge of regret I must confess — after one year and some months as a citizen soldier. What youth will do for love!

I never got back to the Battery (even now, I like to think, to its great loss). In the First World War a few years later, I served with another branch of the Forces for four and a half years, and many were the times during those stormy and dangerous years that I wished I could do what those dear old sergeants, now both dead, made me do so long before — hand in my uniform.

The years sped on and my next association with the Drill Hall was during the last war when I joined the local Home Guard which had its headquarters there, and served for four and a half years. During that time as a Sergeant, I took my turn every nine days in taking out a night guard of 20 men to protect the pipelines at the Swinsty and Fewston Reservoirs. In addition we did training and arms drill at the Drill Hall on most evenings a week. My wife was also, for a period, in charge of the canteen there, with Mrs. Norah Hall and Mrs. Kathleen Whitaker. So after 200 years the old place fulfilled its destiny and was destroyed to make way for progress.

The two Newall Halls

Newall Old Hall — or Newhall as it was known when a stately mansion many years ago — was a large farm house demolished in 1928 to make room for the Housing Estate built by Otley Council. The centre portion was part of the original building erected in the thirteenth or fourteenth centuries, the

Francis Billam, who resided at the present Hall

Newall Old Hall as it was in medieval times

The Hall as a farmhouse before demolition

two wings having been added when it was renovated and reduced in size about the middle of the 1800's. According to Harry Speight, in his 'Upper Wharfedale" it was, in turn, in the possession of the Kighley, Craven, Proctor, Wilkinson and Fawkes families, but must not be confused with the present Newall Hall which, in the early part of the 19th century, was in the occupation of a family named Ward whose descendents, the Billams, long resided there. The late Mr. Francis Billam, who died in 1807, gave his name to the road running alongside the Hall, now named "Billams Hill". He was a gentleman of a charitable disposition to whose memory there is a tablet in Otley Parish Church. In his home he had a fine collection of stuffed birds and natural history objects, which were eventually presented to the Mechanics' Institute (now the Civic Centre) where they were housed for many years in what is still known as the "Bird Room". Amongst a collection of autographs possessed by Mr. Billam, were letters of Oliver Cromwell, the Stuart Monarchs, and Rev. John Wesley.

Farnley Hall

Farnley Hall

Farnley Hall is one of the most interesting houses in Yorkshire. At every step one is reminded of some stirring event in which its former lords played a part, or of some grand old Yorkshire family with which they were associated ages ago. In the house is a handsomely ornamented embayed window, looking into the flower garden, which was removed there in 1840 from Lindley Hall, the ancient Yorkshire seat of the Palmes. The building houses antiques and curios from every quarter of the globe, being a collection of centuries. A hat is preserved at the Hall which is believed to have adorned Cromwell's massive head, also a sword which is vouched for as having protected his person at the Battle of Marston Moor. There is also a watch of Cromwell's carried by him on the same occasion; a sword which belonged to General Lambert and a letter from Charles the First, dated August 1626 in which His Majesty requests the loan of £13. 6s. 8d. These were known as "Benevolences".

There is a chimney piece with quaint overmantel of oak, made from a bedstead traditionally believed to have been occupied by King James the First when he was on a visit to Hawksworth Hall. The walls of the Music Room are adorned by a great number of paintings of the great Masters, including works by van Dyck, Cuyp, Guido, etc. Also paintings by J. M. W. Turner, R.A. from 1806 to 1830.

The most famous picture ever to be seen at Farnley was the beautifully tranquil "Dortrecht", an oil painting which was specially painted by Turner for Mr. Walter Fawkes. Its correct title was "The Dortrecht Packet Boat

"The Dortrecht Packet Boat Becalmed"
by J.M.W. Turner

Becalmed" and, measuring 62ins x 92ins. it was hung at the Royal Academy in 1818. The colours in the original are exquisite and the detail remarkable. It was sold in 1966 to a firm of London art dealers for a sum not named. It is interesting to note that every Christmas Turner received from his friend and patron, Mr. Walter Fawkes, a goose pie and game. The 25th gift of this nature was already packed for dispatch in 1851 when news came of the death of the artist.

John Ruskin, the famous art critic and philosopher, was often a visitor to Farnley Hall and, when driving to Otley Railway Station after a visit in December 1884, accompanied by Mrs. Ayscough Fawkes, he stopped the carriage in Farnley Lane (about the bottom of Prince Henry Road), and said "Look,

a great admirer of Turner's work and, when staying at Farnley Hall, invariably took one of the painter's water colours to his bedroom each evening on retiring to study it for a while.

There is a paradise of old furniture within Farnley Hall, much of it older than the Jacobean and Georgian types which figure so prominently in antique shops. The collection of old chests is fascinating, from the rude iron-bound receptacle with big hinges and many locks, in which Falçasius de Farnley may have kept his title deeds, to the architecturally modelled box of the Rococo period, or the delicately inlaid bit of Sheraton work.

It has been my privilege to visit Farnley Hall several times during my lifetime, the last occasion being in 1946 when a large party of Royal Canadian

The view seen by Ruskin

R.C.A.F. flying personnel

a perfect Turner painting." Mrs. Fawkes wrote afterwards that, engraved on her memory, was the familiar view of Otley Bridge, the River Wharfe gleaming in the veiled sunshine, a soft mist half hiding the town, and the great hill rising slate-coloured above the mist in a luminous sky — just the sort of effect the great artist loved to paint, and had learned to love at Farnley. Ruskin was

Air Force personnel, all flyers, were invited to look round. Major Horton Fawkes kindly allowed me to be present and I was photographed with them afterwards on the steps overlooking the terrace.

The Fawkes family of Farnley Hall have, over the years, been public bene-factors to the people of the Otley district. When the Cemetery in Pool Road was constructed, round about 1860, the land on which the fine en-

41

trance avenue was laid out was donated by Mr. Walter Fawkes.

Entrance avenue to the Cemetry

About the same period, when the Workhouse at Newall (now the Wharfedale General Hospital) was erected, the land for this was also given. Included in the gift was the stone to erect the building, from the Haddockstones Quarry at Clifton, which belonged to the Fawkes' estate.

Wharfemeadows Park at Otley, publicly opened in 1924, comprised land on the river bank extending from the Bridge to Haslingford down the Sand-

Feeding time for swans in Wharfemeadows Park

beds — a distance of one and a half miles — and included some 60 acres. The Park is delightfully situated, the lay-out not spoiling the natural beauty which already existed. Part of the land, the portion near the Bridge, was purchased from Major F. H. Fawkes; and that from the Damstones to the Woods near the Farnley Estate Entrance gates, some 20 acres, was given by him. The rest of the land was rented on lease for twenty-five years, with option to renew, but as it was taken for food production by the Government during the 1939-45 war, and never returned, the lease was not renewed, but allowed to lapse. Thus Otley lost a wonderful sports centre, which had just begun to be developed. Part of it has since been acquired by the West Riding County Council and made into a sports ground for the scholars of Prince Henry's School nearby.

Major Fawkes supplemented his gift by dedicating land at Newall as a playground for children, which he equipped with swings etc., at his own expense; and also donated the site for the Newall Sunday School nearby, which was built from stone from the old Newall Hall.

In 1946 Major L. G. G. W. Horton-Fawkes, O.B.E., presented to Otley about 263 acres of land on East Chevin, including the Danefield Wood Estate and the Deer Park above Caley. This was for the benefit of people of the town and as a memorial to those who gave their lives in the 1939-45 war. This gentleman has also, on several occasions since, made gifts of trees to be planted in the Woods which, under the Council's forestry staff, have become one of the most visited places in the county.

Farnley Church was restored about 1851. Formerly a Chapel of Ease to Otley Parish Church, it contains an interesting West Window on which are engraved the Arms of most of the Kings of England.

Farnley Church

Weston Hall

In 1224, Weston was held by William-de-Stopham, and afterwards passed by marriage into the family of Vavasour. For more than five centuries the house was the ancestral home of the Vavasours, and was maintained in the male line until 1833 when, by the death of William Vavasour, it descended to the Rev. John Carter of Lincoln, Vicar of Weston, who married Ellen, the only sister and heiress of William Vavasour. It then passed to the Dawson's through the marriage of Emma Carter to Christopher Holdsworth Dawson, of Rhoyds Hall, Low Moor. It thus appears that the manor and estate of Weston have never once been sold but have descended by the marriage and inheritance of its various owners from the Norman Conquest to the present time.

In the gardens is a large and highly finished detached Banqueting Hall of three stages and an upper turret. It dates from the time of King Charles the First, and the stonework is embellished

Weston Hall

43

The Dragon Room

Weston Church

with the arms of the Vavasour and Stanley families. Perhaps the most notable apartment in Weston Hall is that known as the "Dragon Room". It dates from the period between the middle of the reigns of Henry the Seventh and Henry the Eighth. The ceiling of the room, studded with small dragons, lions, greyhounds and other devices, has been left untouched in its essential details since this part of the house was built. In the corner can be seen the four-poster bed on which General Fairfax was reputed to have slept, prior to the Battle of Marston Moor in June, 1664.

Weston Church is charmingly situated near the Hall. It is an ancient but unpretentious fabric with a Norman nucleus, witness a small Norman window on the South Nave, and a Chancel Arch of the plainest possible type. The Dawson Chapel contains a tomb to Sir William Stopham, Knight, living in 1312, and there is also a Memorial altar tomb to William Vavasour who died in 1887.

The ruins of Dob Park Castle mark the Northern verge of the Forest of Knaresborough and are thought to be the ruins of one of the three Hunting Lodges or Castelets connected with the preservation of deer and other wild animals of the chase. The other two were John O'Gaunt's Castle and Padside Hall. There is supposed to be a spectral hound guarding a treasure placed in the Castle when the Vavasours were the owners.

Ruins of Dob Park Castle

The Old Inns

The Inns of an old market town, with their traditional backgrounds, and variety of names, make a fascinating study, and it is surprising how many of Otley's have disappeared during the past 70 or so years.

There was the Grey Horse in Kirkgate, the Waterloo in Gay Lane, The Carpenters Arms (afterwards known as the Wharfedale) in Boroughgate, the King's Arms in Bondgate, the Green Man in Kirkgate, the Blue Bell and

The old Black Horse Hotel, in front stand (from left) Mr. Fred Cobley, Mr. T. G. Dawson and his son

The Royal White Horse Hotel

The Blue Bell, with local worthies

46

The Black Bull

Royal White Horse in Manor Square, the Traveller's Rest and the Leeds House in Market Place, the Star in New Market, the Royal Oak in Clapgate, the Half Moon in Beech Hill, and the Cock and Bottle in Bondgate.

The Black Horse was formerly the Coach Inn, and both it and the White Horse were posting houses. Concerning the latter – in the year 1876, H.R.H. the Duke of Connaught visited Otley with his regiment, and an address was presented to him by the Chairman of the Local Board. He stayed at the White Horse Inn, which afterwards secured "letters patent" to use the Royal Coat of Arms, and prefix the word "Royal".

Possibly the palm for age in the hostelries in the town goes to the Black Bull, and it is on record that a party of Cromwell's Ironsides called there for refreshment in 1648, and drank the place dry.

The Bowling Green Hotel was built in 1757 as a Court House, but became unsuitable after a few years and was used for concerts and plays, being then known as the Assembly Rooms until 1825, when it became an Inn.

In the Half Moon the Otley Lodge of Freemasons (one of the oldest in the world) used to hold its meetings about 1760.

It is a long time since the following nonsense about Otley's public houses, printed on a postcard, was first sold in stationers' shops, but occasionally a copy turns up and causes some amusement.

"Having an hour to spend in Otley the other evening I thought I would take a ramble round the town, and my attention was immediately attracted by a beautiful SUMMER CROSS upon which THREE HORSE SHOES were nailed, guarded by a RED LION, which stood near a FOUNTAIN, where a groom named GEORGE, wearing a BLUE BELL in his coat, who came from the MANOR HOUSE, called the WHARFEDALE, was giving a WHITE HORSE, a BAY HORSE and a BLACK HORSE a drink; while a handsome WHITE SWAN, NEW INN the water, was swimming gracefully about. Turning round, I saw a WHEATSHEAF, standing under the shade of a splendid ROYAL OAK, which sheltered the LEEDS HOUSE. Hearing a shout, I looked up and saw a man who had stolen a ROSE AND CROWN bearing the stamp of the QUEEN'S HEAD, running across the BOWLING GREEN pursued by a crowd of people and a butcher with a BLACK BULL. He tried to effect a JUNCTION with his mate, a conjuror, who was juggling with two CROSS PIPES and a COCK AND BOTTLE, but failing in his attempt ran straight into the MASON'S ARMS, who was coming out of the DRAMSHOP with a heavy WOOLPACK on his shoulders made from the FLEECE of a prize sheep; and with the sound of the RING O'BELLS ringing merrily in my ears, I retired to rest aided by the light of the HALF MOON and the evening STAR."

DICK SUMNER

Colourful Characters

With the abolition of Poor Law, the closing down of model lodging houses, and the advent of social security, the colourful and unusual characters one met in the past seem nowadays non-existent. Such as, for instance, Neddy Emmott, an inmate of the Workhouse for 40 years, being admitted in 1873. He used to be in charge of the hand cart which distributed the firewood chopped by the Workhouse inmates, and sold in the town. Neddy was supposed to be a bit daft because, when folk offered him the choice of one of the small silver threepenny pieces which were withdrawn from circulation several years ago, and a copper penny, he always chose the penny. Neddy knew, however, that if he had chosen the silver coin, the offer would not have been repeated. "Moth-

"Mothballs"

balls" was a familiar sight a few years ago, with his trousers tied up with string and decked out with ribbons.

The laziest man Otley ever produced was "Billy Backwater", who lived in the town at the turn of the century. Named William Metcalfe, he was a man of ability and had travelled extensively

"Billy Backwater"

in America and elsewhere, in his youth. He used to say that it was a pity if Otley could not keep one "gentleman". A commercial traveller one day saw him lounging against the Junction Inn, with his hands in his pockets, and enquired the way to the railway station. Billy, without speaking, nodded his head in the required direction. "Well," said the traveller, "if ever I come across a lazier man than you, I'll give you two-pence." Billy, taking one hand out of a pocket said, "Put it in here." It was too much trouble to put the money in himself!

One of the quaintest Otley characters of many years ago was old Balse Bradley, and numerous anecdotes are told of his resource and cunning. One day Balse thought out a scheme for a cheap dinner. He went into the shop of

Mr. W. S. Greaves, a grocer at the top of Bridge Street, and asked "Have you any good hams?" "Yes," said the grocer "there are none better to be had anywhere." "Well, let's have a look at one," said Balse, so Mr. Greaves lifted one down, and handed it to him. Balse first looked it over, reckoned to feel its weight and then, pulling a wooden skewer out of his capacious pocket stuck it well into the ham. Smelling at the skewer he said, "It's bad, it's bad." "Nay," said the grocer, "I haven't such a thing as a bad ham in the shop." "Well," said the rascal, "smell this," at the same time putting the skewer to Mr. Greaves' nose. "It certainly seems to be going a bit," reluctantly admitted the latter. "I'll give you a penny a pound for the ham," said Balse. "All right," said the grocer. "It weighs 30 pounds, and you can have it for 2/6d. It afterwards leaked out that the old reprobate had buried the skewer in a manure heap for a fortnight. The ham was as sound as could be.

The last thatched cottage in Otley was in Walkergate. It belonged to Mr. John Lawson, and eventually became so dilapidated that the Local Board of Health ordered him to pull it down. At one period a character named old "Pauge" lived there. He was an ostler at the Royal White Horse Hotel and a bit of a humorist. On one occasion a commercial traveller stayed at the hotel overnight, and gave "Pauge" instructions to have his horse saddled at 7.30 the next morning. This "Pauge" did, but put the saddle on back to front. "What have you done that for?" said the bewildered man. "Well, sir," replied the ostler, "you never said where you were going; I didn't know whether it was Harrogate or Bradford!"

Memories of Dr. Bennett, for many years a medical practitioner in Otley prompt the following yarn, for the doctor was noted as a bit of a wag. When a little girl swallowed a sixpence, the mother rushed her to Dr. Bennett, who enquired what was wrong. "She's swallowed a sixpence," said the distracted parent. "What shall I do?" "Well," said he, "It's no use bringing her here so take her t'Wesleyan's — it's said they can get brass out of owt." After his retirement, Dr. Bennett lived out of town, and on one of his infrequent visits he met Mr. David Johnson, for many years a joiner and undertaker, who was also a comic. "Well, Johnson," said the Doctor, "How's things?" "Noan so good sin tha left," was the reply as the undertaker turned away.

The last thatched cottage in Otley

Old Otley Families

This photograph of the Otley of bygone days, when it really was a market town in the true sense of the words, and the "Metropolis of Wharfedale" is, I think, worthy of reproduction. Taken in 1883, it is a remarkable view of the top of Boroughgate where it joins Kirkgate and Manor Square, with the shops decorated in honour of Queen Victoria's son and his wife, their Royal High-nesses Prince Leopold and Princess Helen, the Duke and Duchess of Albany, who were staying at Farnley Hall as the guests of Ayscough Fawkes, Esq., on the occasion of a visit to Leeds Musical Festival.

A local committee arranged special public decorations in the town for the distinguished party — including two

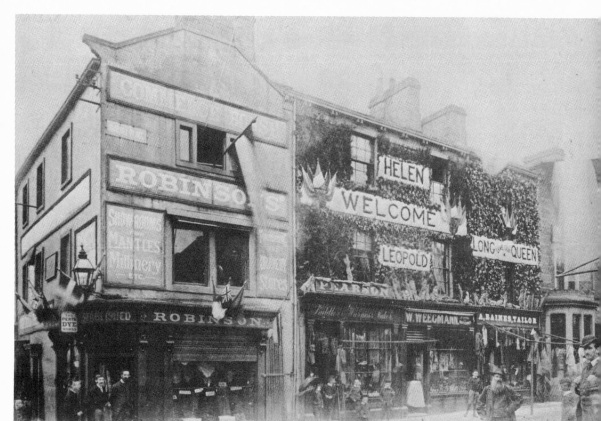

Junction of Boroughgate, Kirkgate and Manor Square

Triumphal Arch at the entrance to the bridge

Triumphal Arches in Bridge Street. All the expenses were borne by public subscription. The Royal signatures in the Parish Church Register make a memorable record of the occasion.

The buildings in the photograph, which appear to be of early nineteenth

Triumphal Arch at the top of Bridge Street

century origin, are of sturdy appearance. At the extreme right of the picture can be seen the old George Inn, which became redundant before the first world war. Baines, a tailor, who occupied the shop next door, was known locally as "Buttony", and some of his descendants now have a garage and engineering works in Harrogate.

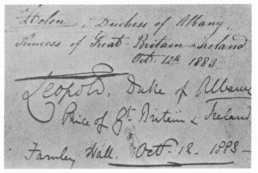

Royal signatures in the Parish register

The next shop is where the German immigrants, William Christian Weegmann and his wife, established their pork butchering business about 1886. Mrs. Weegmann is standing in the doorway. The business is still carried on today in the same name and in the same shop, but under different ownership. R. S. Pearson, a saddler and harness maker, was the occupier of the next door premises, but when he subsequently transferred his business to a shop near the bottom of Beech Hill, Mrs. Fieldhouse, a milliner and fancy draper, took the shop.

"Commerce House" at the end of the block which also extended into Manor Square, was a drapery, millinery and ladies' outfitting business, which included showrooms for the trying on of "mantles", a word long since discarded by the trade. I have been told that two brothers named Robinson founded the firm about 1857. They were both ardent members of the congregation of the old New Connexion Chapel in Westgate. In the photograph one of these brothers — William — can be seen standing in the doorway with his son, William L., who succeeded to the business in 1893.

My father used to tell of another Robinson — "Clogger" Tom — who worked for Mr. Robert Dibb and made clogs in a building in Bondgate, on the site of which now stand the Fire Station premises. After leaving Mr. Dibb's employ, "Clogger" Tom started in another line of business, and on going to Morecambe for his summer holiday he signed his name in the visitors' book thus: "Thos. Robinson, M.D., Otley." Another visitor from the neighbourhood could not make this out, and said to him, "I did not know there was a medical gentleman of the name of Robinson at Otley. In what part of the town is your practice?" "Well," said Tom, "I'm not a medical man, the initials mean 'muffin dealer'!"

Another family of Robinson was so large that a verse was composed of their names which ran:

"There were Joshua, Caleb, Lot and Dan:
Faith, Ruth, Kate and Ann,
Timothy, Job and Peter;
And then came Paul to crown them all."

Mr. Watkinson (Waky) Robinson, a farmer at Dob Park, was a noted elocutionist, and I well remember how thrilled I was as a boy when I heard him recite, attired in complete jockey's outfit including riding whip, "Kissing Cup's Race for the Golden Cup", as an interlude at my father's lecture on "Old Otley" in the Mechanics Institute in 1904. I could almost visualize the snorting animal thundering down the track to victory!

Old Worthies

This photograph taken many years ago, shows that the Buttercross has always, over the years, been a popular and democratic rendezvous for old Otleyites. In those days, of course, just as it was considered "not quite the thing" for women to drink in public houses, so it was out of the question for them to sit in the Buttercross, whereas nowadays there are often to be seen more women than men sitting there.

Another change in custom to be noted is the fashion in beards. In those days the "old uns" sported the face fungus, whereas the present trend is for many young people who wish to be "with it" to have beards, whilst the old age pensioner is usually clean shaven.

The building behind the Butter-cross is the old Leeds House public house and refreshment rooms, the licence of which was surrendered in 1962. Otley Council bought the premises and it is now a restaurant. The building on which the notice board is fixed was where the market stalls were stored, demolished when Moss & Sons built the second stage of their grocery store.

Although I knew most of the characters pictured, curiously enough, after all these years, I can only name a few. I seem to recognise, on the front seat, behind the pillar on the far left of the picture, the face of Mr. W. Clough, a noted bellringer at the Parish Church who, in his time, took part in much change ringing. The third man from Mr. Clough is Mr. Peter Patrick, founder of the former Otley joinery works. The white-bearded person on the front seat, behind the second pillar, is Mr. T. G. Dawson, eldest son of the founder of the printing machine industry in Otley, who lived in Beech Hill.

Of the two figures standing on the pavement, the one on the right was known as "Tommy Nowt"; I don't recall his name, but I have heard my father say that Tommy, after being a heavy drinker for many years, "signed the pledge", and used to go round in the Friendly Societies Association annual procession with a barrel around him, the two ends of which had been knocked out, denoting that he could now see through his folly.

Buttercross

53

When the Railway Came

I cannot resist a nostalgic reference to Otley Railway Station, which was closed and demolished when the railway line between Arthington and Ilkley was discontinued.

When the Leeds and Thirsk railway was opened, after the completion of the Bramhope Tunnel in 1850, the station at Arthington was nearer the village and main road than it is now. In later years it was suggested to take a branch line from this station to Ilkley, through the centres of Pool, Otley and Burley-in-Wharfedale where the stations would have been situated. This proposal did

The station

The station

not meet with the approval of the owners of the estates from whom the necessary land would have had to be purchased, as they wanted the rolling stock
to be as far away from their residences
as possible. They, therefore, refused to
sell the land required unless the track
was constructed nearer the base of
Chevin. So the station at Arthington
had to be moved nearer the Bramhope
Tunnel, and the track constructed from
there. It was completed and opened in
1864, with the result that the stations
of the places I have mentioned were
sited a long way from the town centres,
with consequential inconvenience to the
inhabitants for the next hundred years.

In a separate part of Otley churchyard, in Church Lane, near the Kirkgate
Arcade, is the splendid Memorial to the
23 men who lost their lives during the
construction of the Bramhope Tunnel
on the Leeds to Thirsk railway during
1845-50. Unfortunately, it was made
of soft Caen stone and has not with-
stood the weather.

Bramhope memorial in the churchyard

55

Oldest Show in England

Fountain Hotel, decorated for 100th anniversary of the Show, 1898.

The Wharfedale Agricultural Show is held in Otley early in May each year, and is the oldest show in England. It was founded in 1799. It is also the first show of the season, where stock is generally tried out. When these shows were first instituted they were for the purpose of stimulating and improving stock, but in later years domestic animals were included and became some of the main features. Leaping and Sheep Dog Trials have also attracted interest, and in recent years Rodeos and other novelties have been added.

One of the competitors at the first Otley Show was Mr. Nathaniel Dawson, some of whose descendents still live in the town. The "Leeds Intelligencer" of 1774 had a paragraph to the effect that: "Mr. Nathanial Dawson, an eminent butcher, was married at Otley to Miss Richardson, an agreeable young lady with a handsome fortune."

An amusing anecdote of many years ago concerns the Show. An

Mr. Nathaniel Dawson

56

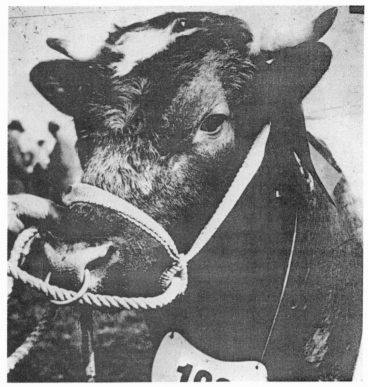

Pat, the Giant Ox

officer of the Yorkshire Yeomanry, whilst congratulating one of the troops on its smart appearance, made a stirring allusion to the medals worn by some of the regular ex-Army veterans in the ranks. On the next parade, another of the men, a native of Wharfedale, appeared with several medals on his chest. Said the officer, "I didn't know you had been in the Regulars." "No, I even't," said the man. "Well, how about the medals then, my good fellow; they can't be yours?" He promptly replied, "Can't they? Ay, but they be. My old coo won 'em all at Otla' Show."

A competitor at Otley Show in 1912 was Pat, the famous Irish-born Yorkshire-reared Giant Ox, which weighed 254 stones, and was said to be the biggest in the world. His preserved head is in York Castle Museum.

Currier - Cabinet Minister

"There's nothing like leather" is a trite old saying, but in Otley before the founding of the printing machine industry, it was something more than that for, to a great extent, the prosperity of the town depended on that trade. Tanyards and curriers' shops abounded in almost every part of the district — in fact the former name of "Paradise Square", off Walkergate and Charles Street, now a car park after the houses were demolished, was formerly "Tanner's Fold".

57

From the tanyards of Otley, over the years, have gone men of whom the town may be justly proud. One such character was William Lawies Jackson, whose life story under the heading, "From Tanyard to the House of Lords" if written should prove an inspiration to the present and future generations.

William (Bill) Jackson

Robert Barker, founder of the old tannery, with his wife.

The old tanyard in Bondgate, Otley, was founded and carried on for many years by Mr. Robert Barker, grandfather of Mr. William H. Barker, J.P., who will be well remembered by older people in the town as the immaculate chairman of the Otley Bench of Magistrates for many years; and also as a former Chairman of Otley Urban District Council, on which one of his sons, Mr. Tom Barker, also served as member and chairman in later years.

The present directors of the leather firm of Messrs. William Barker and Sons, Ltd., in Cross Green, are also descendents of Mr. Robert Barker, as was also Capt. Norman L. Barker, O.B.E., who had distinguished careers in the Army,

where he was mentioned in despatches during the 1914-18 war, and in the National Fire Service for 25 years, where for most of the time he was Chief of the Otley Fire Brigade.

For his working foreman, Mr. Robert Barker had a man named William Jackson — known as Bill — who was of a convivial nature, so much so that he spent most of his money at the Woolpack Inn instead of taking it home to his hard-working and patient wife who had to take in washing to eke out the meagre family income.

It is not surprising, therefore, that poverty and want were to be found in the home. Bill and his wife lived in a mean cottage in a yard off Kirkgate, then known as Bullock Fold, where cattle were formerly kept before being sent to one of the numerous slaughterhouses in the vicinity. This yard, where Mr. Joseph Barber established his tobacco factory, was afterwards known for many years until it was demolished as Barber's

Yard. Messrs. Woolworth's store now stands on the site.

In this environment, in 1840, was born Bill Jackson's only son, William Lawies who, as he grew older, came to know what poverty and want meant. Brighter days were in store, however, for old Robert Barker signed the pledge and persuaded all his workmen to do the same. In consequence, as circumstances improved, Bill Jackson and his family left Bullock Fold to live in a house near the grocery shop of Mr. Robert Richardson at the corner of Kirkgate and Bondgate (now rebuilt and the premises of Messrs. H. J. Waye and Son Ltd., the travel agents). Mrs. Jackson continued to take in washing as of yore, when she had to provide the necessities of life for young William and herself, but now the money was for a definite purpose – Bill Jackson had determined to become master of his own business, and his wife did all she could to assist him.

The years rolled on, and William Jackson at last achieved his desire and took a tanyard at Headingley, near Leeds, but through adverse circumstances was forced to call his creditors together. This gave his son, young William Lawies, a purpose in life, which was to pay all his father's debts in full and create a successful business.

Having succeeded in business, Mr. Jackson now turned his attention to local politics, and gained a seat on Leeds City Council where he did useful service and became Lord Mayor. Asked to stand for Parliament, he was elected by a large majority to represent Leeds.

In Parliament, as in business and municipal politics, Mr. Jackson's progress was rapid, and he was soon included in the Cabinet as one of the most able men in the country. He was Financial Secretary to the Treasury for several years, and Chief Secretary for Ireland in 1891-2. He was appointed to preside over the committee which enquired into the notorious raid into the Transvaal in 1895 by Sir Leander Starr Jameson, who subsequently received ten months' imprisonment in London for that escapade.

An active and distinguished chairman of the former Great Northern Railway Company, Mr. Jackson was, for his services, raised to the Peerage in King Edward VII's Coronation year, and became the first Baron Allerton.

Lord Allerton

Lord Allerton was most retiring in his high position. My father once wrote to him asking for particulars of his early struggles. He received the following reply: "As it is turned 60 years since I left Otley, I cannot give you any information of my life in the town that would be of any interest; the main fact in the Otley connection is that I got from it the best wife any man ever had."

Lord Allerton's wife was a sister of Mr. James Tempest founder of a but-

Mr. James Tempest

The Hon. F. S. Jackson

birth. One of Lord Allerton's sons was the Hon. F. S. Jackson, M.P., the well known Yorkshire County cricketer, who played during the time of the captaincy of Lord Hawke. Later, as Sir Stanley Jackson, he became Governor of Bengal. It was in 1902, I think, that an Australian cricket team toured Britain, and played against a Yorkshire side at Headingley, Leeds. At that time the Hon. F. S. Jackson was in his "prime" as a Yorkshire player — in fact he was considered to be the best amateur ever to turn out for the county — and was included in the team. Australia batted first and scored 150 runs in the first innings, but they got Yorkshire out for 125. In the second innings F. S. Jackson and the great George Hirst between them dismissed Australia for 25 runs. This left only 51 runs to get to win the match, which Yorkshire did for the loss of five wickets! A wonderful achievement.

chering business carried on for over 100 years in Otley in premises in Boroughgate. There are still members of the family in the town, one of whom, Mr. Charles Gerald Tempest, is managing director of the ironmongery business in Market Place founded by his grandfather, Mr. Charles R. Tempest, in 1891.

My father privately thought that perhaps there was another reason for Lord Allerton's reluctance to give particulars of his early life in Otley. On one occasion, whilst he was Chief Secretary for Ireland, he came to address a meeting in the town, and was given a rough reception by the Irish community living here, many of whom were descendents of the families brought over to Otley at the time of the potato famine in 1847 and who were clamouring for Home Rule in Ireland. At any rate, he never again addressed a meeting in the town of his

Lost Industries

At one time, many Otley families brewed their own ale, and there were numerous malt kilns. There were also brewers and coopers, the last brewer being Mr. G. A. Robinson, of the Cross Pipes Inn, and the last cooper Mr. J. Whitaker, in Market Street.

Another important industry, lost to the town, was the manufacture of bricks for building purposes. Mr. Thomas F. Marshall, who resided at Chevin Hall, which he built, had a kiln in a field at the end of Birdcage Walk, near the bottom of West Chevin Road, and it was there that the bricks were made for a culvert from Station Road, down Kirkgate and Bridge Street, to take sewage into the river. This was the first drainage scheme carried out by the Local Board of Health, after the adoption of the Public Health Act, about 1871.

Another kiln was built down East Busk Lane which, at the time of the Civil War, was the highway to Wetherby and York, and along which Prince Rupert is supposed to have passed on his way to the Battle of Marston Moor in 1644. A field in which he camped for the night is still called locally, "Camp Field". This kiln in East Busk Lane was erected by Benjamin Harrison, a farmer, who lived at Midgley Farm and whose brother emigrated to North America where he became of such importance that one of his sons, General Harrison, eventually became President of the U.S.A. Benjamin Harrison had a family of eight children, and when he died he left nearly £5,000 to be divided amongst them. The brickmaking business had been so successful, up to his decease, that two of his sons, who were twins — Benjamin and Joseph — thought there was more to be made out of bricks than by farming, and with their shares of the legacy they purchased a large piece of land off the new road just opened to Leeds, near Cambridge, in which they erected several large kilns to make bricks in a scientific way, by patent machinery — bricks not of clay, but of shale. They expected to make a fortune in a short time, but alas for human expectations, became bankrupt instead. The site was eventually filled in with good soil and a garden developed by Mr. Phil S. Wade. A residence has since been erected there.

Other lost industries of Otley are the manufacture of woollen cloth, for which the water of the river was specially suited, giving the cloth a brighter colour and a softer feel to the hand; weaving, stocking-making, dyeing, case clock making (super craftsmen were the Roberts Brothers who had a shop in Market Place about the end of the eighteenth century, and specialised in engraved brass dials), tobacco blending, basket making, corset and stay making, the designing and making of washing and wringing machines and also printers' sundries by William Dawson; organ making, Valentine card printing, beaver hat making, rope and twine walking (a Rope Walk was in Bondgate, on the site of the present Fire Station) clog making, bit and stirrup making by Mr. William F. Longfield at the old Silver Mill in Leeds Road, where quoits — as used in the ancient game — were also made; and the manufacture of musical instruments in a shop in New Market by Mr. G. D. Wigglesworth, in 1860. The making of guns, for which he became noted in the district, was carried on in New Cross many years ago by Mr. Francis Whitley. There is a specimen of his craft in the Museum of Otley.

Ancient Customs

The Maypole. 1900

Many an ancient custom was enacted in the old town in by-gone days. There was the horn blowing (a close of land called "Bugle Ing" is situated between West Busk Lane and the Wharfe). The last horn blower was Mr. Nicholson, who got the workpeople at Messrs. Ackroyd's Mill up at 5.30 a.m. each day by blowing the horn.

Other activities included Easter and wedding customs, St. Valentine's day celebrations, Christmas and New Year masquerades, riding the stang (the effigy usually being burned in Cross Green), bull-baiting, cock fighting (in which the neighbouring gentry took a great delight), badger baiting, otter hunting, and quoits and knur and spell competitions on Pisgah Hill. In the old days, knocking on the doors of neighbours and bidding them to a funeral, was a common practice.

Up to the beginning of the present century Otley always commemorated the ushering in of blooming May, and certain it is that there was a Maypole to dance around in the days of the "Merry Monarch". The present shaft is the fifth to be erected in the past 200 years, one of its predecessors being shattered by lightning in 1871.

Mr. Nicholson

Memories of Two Chemists

The closing down of the business of Messrs. Fairfax Fearnley Ltd., at the corner of Manor Square and Clapgate, Otley, marked the end of an era, for retail trading in pharmaceutical and kindred goods had been carried on in those premises for well over a hundred years.

In my young days, the business was in the hands of Mr. Richard Pratt, a kindly and courteous gentleman, who came to Otley from Norfolk in 1855,

Richard M. Pratt, a keen fisherman

and went to his eternal rest in the year 1917 at the ripe old age of 89 years.

For most of the time he lived in Otley he resided in the bottom house of East View Terrace, which was then considered one of the "class" districts of the town. He had a deep and abiding interest in the affairs of Otley, and the well-being of its people, particularly matters affecting the Parish Church, where he was a Churchwarden for many years, at the same time as Mr. Fred Payne.

He was, moreover, a very enterprising business man and shopkeeper in the days when doctors mostly made up their own prescriptions, although I did notice that a local guide book of 1890 I was once perusing contained a full-page advertisement of Richard M. Pratt, which stated, "Physicians' prescriptions and family recipes carefully prepared with drugs of warranted purity". Much of his trade, however, centred around remedies of his own concoction and some of them make very interesting reading.

For instance, we learn that Pratt's Domestic Aperient Pills were for billiousness and liver complaints, at 7½d. and 1/1½d. a box; Pratt's Orange Quinine Wine was an excellent tonic for weak and delicate persons; Pratt's Baking Powder was for making unfermented bread, teacakes, pastry, puddings, etc., producing a more wholesome and easily digested article of diet, with half the usual quantity of butter and eggs.

He was the sole proprietor of the great Yorkshire Tic and Toothache Remedy, the use of which resulted in a permanent and effectual cure (but only if the simple directions given with each box are followed); Walker's Chinese Pills should be used by all suffering from billious complaints, indigestion, sick headaches, giddiness, skin eruptions and so forth. There were also tobaccos, cigars and fancy snuffs for sale — but no mention of cigarettes!

64

Mr. Pratt was an enthusiastic fisherman and there was hardly a "reach" on the River Wharfe on either side of the Bridge which was not known to him. In this connection a story used to be told about he and old Balse Bradley, a

Balse Bradley

noted Otley "character" of that time, who "lived on his wits", some of whose exploits I have related elsewhere in this book. One day Balse happened to be in the shop of Mr. Pratt when a lad came in who lived at Storrith's Farm (where the Otley Golf Links now are). "I hope they haven't poisoned that beck again this year," said Mr. Pratt to the lad. It was the trout breeding season and the beck in question was Mickle Ing, where the fish were accustomed to "spawn". "I don't know," said the lad, "but I saw two dead fish," and the chemist, sending for them, confirmed that they had indeed been poisoned. The old chap left the shop, ostensibly to dispose of them by burning. He returned, however, a short time afterwards and requested the

loan of Mr. Pratt's landing net. "What do you want it for?" asked the chemist, but all Balse would say was that he would return it. In the meantime, the old rascal had been to see Mr. Dale, who kept the Black Horse Hotel, and said to him, "I've two nice trout here which I have caught this morning; will you give me eighteen pence for them?" "I'll give you a shilling," replied the publican. "No", said Balse, "I can't take a shilling but as you have always been a friend to me and done me many a good turn you can have them for fourteen pence," and he actually got 1/2d. for the poisoned fish!

Balse was noted for his illegal fishing, but was too canny ever to get caught. On one occasion he had gone to "Foster's Holme", up Burley Road, to poach in the river, when he saw two strangers fishing in the very "reach" he intended trying. He always wore a brown velveteen coat, such as old-time gamekeepers used to wear, and anyone not knowing him would take him for a member of that fraternity. Going up to the men, Balse said to one of them, "Do you know you are trespassing; I must take your names?" "If we go", the man replied, "I suppose it will be all right?" "No", said Bradley, "I must have your names; I've been looking for you for a long time." Having given their names the men packed up and departed, whereupon Balse sat down and fished the "reach" they had left. He was not only trespassing himself, but poaching as well!

Another chemist in business in Manor Square in the early years of this century, whom I remember well, was Mr. Joseph Hamond, and in my memory I can still visualise the big coloured glass bottles displayed in his shop window. He was a very pleasant man and a pillar of the Otley Congregational Church where, I think, he held the office of Deacon. He was, however, when I was an apprentice printer, with my father, the bane of my life, for he was an extremely erratic writer. Mr. Hamond often advertised in the local magazines we printed, and my father always gave me the "copy" to set into type. And what a job I did have, for he would commence writing in the top left hand corner of the sheet and finish up in the bottom right hand one. When I protested I couldn't read the "copy", my father always trotted out the same old tale.

It seems that before he commenced business on his own, about 1894, he worked as a journeyman compositor for several years on the "Bradford Telegraph". On the staff there was an old compositor who claimed he could read any "copy" ever sent in — nothing was too difficult — and so the other men thought they would try him out. After sticking a fly in a bottle of ink, they placed it on a clean sheet of paper, which it soon made a mess of. Presenting the paper to the old chap, they asked him to decipher it. Pulling his glasses from his forehead on to his nose, he turned the paper round and round. Finally, putting it on his "frame" and picking up his "setting stick", he got to work and turned out the finest "leader" on "Political Economy" that paper had ever published!

So related my father. But if he ever thought that story would enable me to read Mr. Hamond's scrawl any better he must have been sadly disappointed, for it never did!

An Old Lintel

Alterations at the car showrooms in Boroughgate of Messrs. Jacksons of Otley Ltd., necessitated the demolition of outbuildings at the rear of the site on which

Dr. Ritchie

stood "Romagna House", pulled down a good few years ago owing to its unsafe condition, but still remembered by an older generation of Otley people as housing the surgeries, in turn, of Drs. Williamson and Wolfe. I believe it was also a former residence of Dr. Ritchie, an Otley medical practitioner, whose son Frank, a noted local athlete and runner, created records over the mile which stood for many years.

These outbuildings were included in the "Romagna House" property, and amongst the stones brought down at the demolition was a carved lintel, bearing the date of 1728. This headstone is of the same Georgian period as one over a dwelling in Crow Lane, which shows the date of 1733, and also one in the wall of the Bowling Green Hotel in Bondgate. It had been made for a much more pretentious building, as it was much longer than the doorway of the outbuilding over which it was fixed, and also the supporting uprights were not in conformity with the period in which it was carved. Most probably it would be from some house fronting Boroughgate, where the best dwellings in the town were situated — perhaps even from the site of the old Wesleyan Chapel adjoining which, built in 1825, now comprises the main showrooms and offices of Messrs. Jackson.

My interest in the stone stems from the initials "I.B." which, in addition to the date, are carved upon it. The apparent "I", of course, is an old Latin "J" — as in "I.H.S." (Jesus Hominum Salvator) — and the name could be that of Jabez Brumfitt, member of a family which, until recent years, was prominent in the affairs of the town and district as property owners, farmers, fell-mongers, curriers, butchers, cattle dealers and publicans amongst other things.

He could also be the son or grandson of a Jabez Brumfitt who, according to Mr. Donald B. Good, was the owner of Whiteley Croft at the time of the Civil War, when King Charles the First was clashing with Parliament. Mr. Good, who has premises in Whiteley Croft, and is a keen student of local history, says that on the first deeds of his property, which date back to the middle of the seven-teenth century, the name of Jabez Brum-fitt is written as being the vendor.

He also says that in a book on the battles of the Civil War, in his possession, it is stated that at the time of the Battle of Marston Moor, in 1644, troopers of Prince Rupert's Horse camped for the night in the "Croft of Whiteley" at Otley, the soldiers being billeted in a large barn, whilst the horses ran in the fields. At that time, Whiteley Croft, which also included an "Upper" and a "Lower", stretched from the base of the Chevin to the walls of

Stone dated 1606

the Parish Church. Across this land ran a beck with an abundant supply of pure water from springs on Chevin which would help to revive the jaded horses after their long treck from Lancashire, hence the reason for using this particular place. This beck is still in existence, but nowadays runs underground in culverts. Passing beneath Station Road, it goes through the old Tanyard and beneath Bondgate on its way to the river.

Incidentally, the oldest date carved on any stone in Otley is on the lintel over a built-up doorway in the outside wall of a joiner's shop in an extension of Courthouse Street. It is near the Mechanics' Institute, and faces the top ends of Hamilton and Ramsey Terraces. The stone bears the date of 1606, together with the initials "I.F." — again the "I" appearing to be an old Latin "J" — which could be those of a member of the influential Foster family which owned the mills and tan pits near the river on the West side of Otley before they were turned over entirely to textiles by Mr. William Ackroyd.

William "Duffit" Thompson

It is said that every decade produces its outstanding personality, and one of the most colourful characters ever to be associated with Otley was William Thompson, who was born in the town in 1824 and died in 1864, after a short but

William "Duffit" Thompson

tempestuous span of life. So full of incident, however, was his career that the recounting of some of the exploits in it will, I think, prove of interest to young and old alike.

Thompson, for some unknown reason known locally as "Duffit", was a step-brother of Mr. Joseph Walsh, a well known Nonconformist of that day, who was a devout supporter of the Otley Wesleyan Methodist Church.

In business Mr. Walsh was in the leather trade — I think he made leather heels wholesale for the boot and shoe

industry — and his business was conducted in the large building near the Maypole which, formerly the printing works of Webb, Millington and Co., is now a series of retail shops. It was in these same premises that in the 1920's his son, Mr. Arthur Walshaw, who followed him in business, installed the first wireless transmitting and receiving set in Otley, the aerial running from his building across to the Maypole. Mr. Joseph Walsh related to my father some of the history of his kinsman, hence this explanation of his identity.

Duffit Thompson, like Simon of old, was a Tanner by trade and worked for Mr. Robert Barker, who had a tanyard in Bondgate when Bill Jackson, father of the first Lord Allerton, was foreman of the yard.

When he was 24, Duffit "packed up" tanning and tramped to London, which took him three days, on the first of which he covered 75 miles! Arriving there, he enlisted in the Royal Horse Guards Blue, and his splendid form and physique becoming developed by military training, he showed off most advantageously the uniform of his regiment, for he stood six feet four inches in his stockinged feet, and weighed between 16½ and 17 stones.

He was, in fact, one of the handsomest men in Queen Victoria's Life Guards, and on one occasion whilst on duty at Windsor Castle as one of the Guards in attendance on his Royal Highness, Prince Albert, the Duke of Wellington was heard to say to the Duke of Cambridge, "When are you going to get me a squadron of men like this one?" pointing at Thompson. To which Cambridge replied, "That is an impossibility!"

After quitting the Army Duffit was sought after by artists and sculptors to

Crossley Statue, People's Park, Halifax

famous artist, and was employed by Sir Edwin Landseer, R.A., in casting the lions for the Statue in Trafalgar Square, London.

Unfortunately, he embarked on a life of dissipation, with wild drinking and gambling, often downing as much as 30 quarts of beer a day. This went on until he was unexpectedly converted in 1864 — one of the most remarkable events of his life — and as he was always the leader in the wild pranks of his youth, so he became a leader in the Church of Christ.

Many stories have been told of the wild escapades of Duffit Thompson in his early days at Otley. At one time he worked for an uncle, a stone mason and builder, and was sent, along with several others into the country where they were erecting some farm buildings. On the way out, in the early morning, Duffit commenced to eat his dinner, which was tied up in a red cotton handkerchief. "Tha'll be 'ungry, mi lad, afore tha gets home, eating thi' dinner now," said one of the men. "Nay ah sarn't," replied the boy, "Ah'll get some dinner reight enuff."

sit as a model, and the statue of Francis Crossley in the People's Park, Halifax, was designed from his stately form. He often sat for Sir John Millais, R.A., the

Thompson preaching in Regent's Park, London

Dinner time came, and with it the spectacle of Duffit chasing an old sow round a field. He had a stick in one hand, and was waving the red cotton handkerchief in the other. This brought out the farmer's wife, who enquired why he was chasing the pig. "Why" said he, "t'beastly thing has eaten all mi dinner." "Niver mind," said the woman, "Come inta t'house an ah'll gie thee a good tuck-in," which she did!

On one occasion, Duffit and his pals took the stall of an Otley butcher and placed it across the ridge of the chancel of Otley Parish Church, where it remained for several days until it was wanted for the weekly market, when the butcher had to give them half-a-crown to get it down. One of their favourite pastimes was to change business signs during the night-time. Thus on the door of Dr. Shaw's surgery in Borough-gate was once seen affixed a notice: "Mangling done here".

Duffit once played the "ghost" in the Parish Churchyard, covered with a cow's skin, including horns and tail; but the last lark he was associated with before leaving Otley — and probably the reason he did so — was the tolling of a bell at the Parish Church during the night. At eight o'clock each evening, it was the custom of the Sexton's son to ring for evensong, and he usually took along a few friends with him for company. One night Thompson went with them, slipped up amongst the bells and quietly tied the end of a piece of string to one of them, putting the other end through the grille in the Tower down to the ground outside. Later that night, accompanied by several of his pals, he tied another piece of string to this and took it across the Churchyard into the field adjoining, from where they started tolling the bell. A great many people were brought out of bed, including the Vicar and the Parish Clerk, but the puzzle was not solved until the next morning when the string was discovered hanging down the church steeple.

Poor Law in the Wharfedale Union

Before the passing of the Poor Law Act in 1861, most townships had their own poorhouse, the one at Otley being situated in Cross Green, on the site of which now stands a car showroom. Underneath the building was the village "keep" where male malefactors were incarcerated, and in the yard behind was the "Pinfold", in which straying sheep and cattle were kept until claimed In my time, Mrs. Sally Denison kept a small sweet shop there, and her father Jim Robinson was the local Pinder. The road at the side is now known as "Denison Hill".

The Poor Law Act brought the Wharfedale Union into being, this comprising 17 townships. The first meeting, at the White Hart Inn, Pool, elected Mr. Matthew Whitaker Thompson as the Chairman of the Board of Guardians.

The Workhouse was at Carlton where the poor were housed in a barrack-like room, and relief to the wife of a pauper

Sally Denison, in the doorway of her shop, which was the old Poor house.

Wharfedale Union workhouse at Newall, now part of the General Hospital

with three children of ten shillings per week was thought to be marvellous generosity.

In 1869 a further 16 townships were admitted to the Wharfedale Union, and as the Carlton place became too small to accommodate the increased number of paupers, the institution at Newall was opened in 1873, the foundation stone being laid two years earlier by Mr. Thomas Denison of Yeadon, then.

Laying the Infirmary foundation stone by Mr. Jonathan Peate

The completed Infirmary

Chairman of the Board of Guardians. The cost of the building was £15,000, with a further sum of £1,400 shortly after, for extension.

A new infirmary to hold 70 beds was added in 1907, and Mr. Jonathan Peate of Guiseley, who was Chairman of the Board from 1898 to the early 1920's laid the foundation stone in 1905. After the ceremony Mr. Peate and Mr. James Lund (Chairman of the House Committee) entertained selected guests to luncheon at the Royal White Horse Hotel, Otley, both men defraying the cost.

Provision was made at the Workhouse, or "Newhall" as it came to be known, for destitute people to live there, the average number of men, women and children permanently accommodated being about 100. In addition, there were casual wards for vagrants or tramps as they were called — both male and female — who travelled from one Workhouse to another. Usually they were admitted about 6 p.m. and given a bath and a meal.

Then, after a night's rest in a wooden bunk with a couple of blankets, they had breakfast and spent the day doing

First nursing staff

72

"task work", which mostly consisted of picking oakum for the making of mats. After another night's rest they were released the next morning and sent on their way with a packet of bread and cheese. I remember seeing them waiting for admission near an old wall just outside the gates. Any small items such as tobacco or a few coppers, they would push into crannies in the wall to prevent them being taken from them by the workhouse officials. These things were retrieved when they were discharged — if they could be found. I know the local kids got many a little windfall at times.

The permanent male inmates had the job of chopping old railway sleepers into firewood, which was sold to the public in bags, and delivered on handcarts. The women helped in the cleaning of the institution, and in the bakery and laundry. Some of the illustrations give an idea of what life was for these poor souls before the days of social security.

Woman vagrant awaiting admission

One of the most colourful characters amongst the inmates I remember was Neddy Emmott, who was there for over 40 years, after being admitted in 1875. At one time a Mr. Mellor was the Master at the workhouse, and on one occasion when Neddy had misbehaved himself the Master, for punishment, locked him in the mortuary, on the slab of which, in its coffin, rested the corpse of another Otley character, old "San Nellie Bob". No sooner had the key been turned than Neddy, with characteristic courage, lifted the body out of the coffin, propped it

Admission gates and casual wards for vagrants

Gentleman of the road arriving in style

73

Sleeping accommodation

"Task work", picking oakum, in return for accommodation

74

Workhouse bakery

Rest room for permanent woman inmates

A permanent woman inmate

Neddy Emmott

Inmates' Christmas dinner served by Guardians in 1898

against the wall with a broomstick and getting into the coffin himself promptly went to sleep, remaining in the mortuary all night. On remembering next morning, Mr. Mellor rushed to the building, opened the door and was petrified to see the corpse standing against the wall; and when Neddy sat up in the coffin saying, "I'm here Maister", you can judge the surprise he got. As Neddy said afterwards, "He wor off dahn't drive wi' his cap off, as if t'devil wor after him."

The man whose body was in the coffin was an old washerman who formerly lived in New Market. His mother, who was also a quaint character, made a precarious living for years selling sand from door-to-door, for sanding the stone floors of kitchens and sculleries, and was nick-named "Sand Nellie". The son's name was Bob, and so he had to be "Sand Nellie's Bob", which was corrupted to "San Nellie Bob".

"San Nellie Bob"

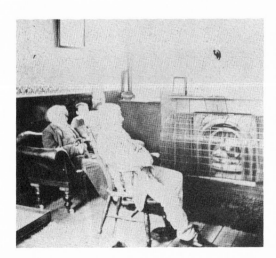

Men's Rest Room

Mr. D.P. Jones, Workhouse Master and Staff 1910.

77

The Garnett Family

Mr. Peter Garnett

There are no longer any members of the paper-making family of Garnett living in Otley — only the name exists at the Wharfeside Mills. In the past, however, they played a major part in the town's affairs, and also made names for themselves in other parts of the country.

The Reverend Richard Garnett, who died in London in 1850, was born in Otley. From being an usher in a school in Southwell, he rose to the important position of Keeper of Printed Books at the British Museum; he was also a distinguished linguist. The same post was also secured by his son, Dr. Richard Garnett, LL.D., C.B., who also contributed articles to Encyclopaedia Britannica and other publications. He also wrote biographies of Carlyle, Milton and Emerson. Dr. Garnett was also a noted member of the Royal Institution of Great Britain.

Mr. Peter Garnett was the first Chairman of the Local Board of Health when it was formed in 1864, and his son, Jeremiah, followed him in that office. This latter gentleman was, according to

Mr. Jeremiah Garnett

The old pig pens in Clapgate, and the Royal Oak Inn about 1880, the Grammar School can be seen in the background.

78

my father, somewhat autocratic in his views, and conscious of his position as one of the town's leading industrialists, but on one occasion he was "taken down a peg or two". The incident, seen by my father, was the presentation in front of the pig market in Clapgate — on the site of which now stands Barclay's Bank — of a silver snuff box to Jim Robinson (usually referred to as "One-armed Jim") who was the Pinder when the Pinfold was situated in Cross Green.

It seems that some of Mr. Jeremiah Garnett's sheep had been found straying on the road and given in charge of the Pinder. On hearing about this, Mr. Garnett sent his clerk to collect them, but gave him no money to pay the fee. Now, Jim could legally detain the animals until this fee was paid, and so the clerk had to leave without them. "I we'ant let 'em go wi'out Mr. Garnett comes his-self an' puts t'money inti mi'and," said he. Ultimately, after about a week, during which time the fee had gradually increased, Mr. Garnett did go himself, paid the money, and collected the sheep. Mr. Clifton Wilkinson, a magistrate, and another leading member of the local gentry, who had heard about the affair, met Robinson one Friday afternoon outside the pig pens. Pulling out his silver snuff box, he

said, "Have a pinch of snuff, James; nay, accept the box as a present. They tell me you have made the proudest man in Otley bend to you."

Mr. H. W. T. (Harry) Garnett, with his brother, Mr. P. P. R. (Percy) Garnett, I remember well as being, in my younger days, connected with the paper mill as principals. The former at one time lived near the mill at a house, "Wharfe-side", now pulled down, whilst the latter resided at Harrogate. Mr. Harry Garnett was a noted rugby football player and one of the personalities of that game. He captained Yorkshire teams from 1873 to 1880, and played for England against Scotland in 1877. He was the first President of the York-shire County Club from 1876 to 1883 and in 1889-90 was President of the Rugby Football Union. He was also President of Otley Rugby Club for many years, including the memorable cup-winning year of 1889, although in his playing days he was a member of the Bradford club, and turned out for them. In his later years he resided in Burley-in-Wharfedale.

Mr. Percy Garnett was a talented tennis player who, I think, assisted the Yorkshire Club in his young days. For many years he was the honorary secre-

Broom Robinson, Harry Shaw and
Jim Robinson with the snuff box

79

tary of a leading Harrogate tennis club.

Both the brothers were men of fine physique and very good swimmers, and used the River Wharfe to indulge in their pastime. It was said — although I, personally, never saw them — that when the river was in "spate", usually at the fall of the year, they went over the weir in a flat-bottomed boat. At times this overturned but such powerful swimmers were they that they were never really in danger.

Mr. Harry Garnett's son, Ray, was a crack shot with a rifle, and often competed at Bisley in the National competitions. He also was a Yorkshire County tennis player. One of Harry's daughters — Maude — was, I remember, a talented contralto singer.

During the period of Mr. Harry Garnett's regime at the paper mill, an Irishman nick-named "Paddy Hoss" was employed there. I don't remember his real name, but he was engaged on such outside jobs as stone walling. On one occasion he was repairing a wall (a rubble one in those days) along the river bank in Mill Lane, which had to be done when the water was low. In a local pub one evening, Paddy was having a drink when an acquaintance asked him if he had been dry-walling. "How the divil can I have been dry-walling," replied the Irishman, "when I've been up to mi knees in wather all the day?" Mr. Garnett kept sheep, and when several of them died Paddy had to bury them. Later, seeing him digging another hole, Mr. Garnett asked what he was doing that for. "Sure sir," said Paddy, "I'm after digging another hole to bury the muck I got out of the first one!"

It was at Garnett's Mill that, many years ago, Mr. Jonas Jowett worked when he saved his first hundred pounds, which was the beginning of a little fortune. Joney, who was a paper maker and never had more than fifteen shillings a week wage, took the money to Mr.

Mr. Jonas Jowett

John Hartley, the miller, to invest for him. "The money looks a queer colour", said Mr. Hartley. "Where have you had it?" "Oh," said Joney, "I've saved it in the hot dyeing liquor vat where I work." Old Charlie Longfield, who worked at the same vat, nearly had a fit when he heard about this. "Only to think how thirsty I've often been," he groaned, "and all that money within reach; I'd had some gills if I'd only known!"

Mr. Jowett used the money he saved to pay the deposit on the two houses he built in Cross Green near the Maypole, which he named "Thorntree Houses". He lived in one of them after retiring from work, but they are now used as offices.

Mr. John Hartley, the corn miller I have mentioned, was always known as "Laddie" Hartley. He had half the premises at Wharfeside which, in fact, had been a corn mill for years before paper-making began there. Mr. Hartley also rented the land at the top of Chevin where he ran sheep, looked after by a shepherd named Myers, who lived in the cottage at the top of the hill. His wife, Jenny, made tea for visitors who came to see the wonderful view, and that is where the name "Jenny's Cottage" originated.

Mr. John Hartley

Wharfeside Mills, when one half was used for cornmilling and the other for papermaking.

81

Memories

of Schooldays

Teaching staff at North Parade School about 1898. Miss Annie Rayner is shown seated in the centre. Mr Edwin Smith is standing at the right.

The theory propounded by many educationists that the early formative years of a child are vital to the amount and quality of the knowledge it acquires in later years is really turning the clock back for, at the tender age of three years, I distinctly remember my mother taking me to the infants' department of the North Parade Board School, where the headmistress, Miss Annie Reyner, enrolled me in the "Baby class". That was the only occasion I was ever accompanied to school by an adult.

We lived in Mount Pisgah, and as most of the other youngsters in the district attended the Mill School in Ilkley Road, I was usually on my own during the four journeys to school and back each day for, of course, there were no school dinners or buses then. Motors being non-existent, traffic hazards were not so great, but with lots of horse-drawn vehicles about things could be pretty terrifying to a child at times, especially when a horse ran away.

One of the memories I have of those early days up and down Westgate is of watching the late Mr. George Arthur Robinson, the landlord of the Cross Pipes Inn, brewing his own beer. He had a long pole with which he used to mix the warm liquid in a big vat, and even after all these years when I pass the building I fancy I can still smell the aromatic aroma of hops and malt. In the old days most of the public houses brewed their own ale, and Mr. Robinson was the last one to do so.

I don't remember a lot about the few years I spent in the Infants' School, except the pot hooks written on the blackboard to teach us how to write, and the Maypole with its coloured ribbons, around which we used to dance on Friday afternoons, before finishing school for the week-end. I think that was the beginning of the love of dancing I have had all my life.

Later on, after I had got into the senior school at North Parade, I became more perceptive. In those days I never had much time for association football, and cricket, I thought, was too slow. This is somewhat surprising because, at the Board School two of the teachers were keen soccer exponents – Mr. L'Estrange Heppard and Mr. Harry Loseby. They used to demonstrate the game in the playground at playtimes. They also trained some very good school-boy teams, which usually won the trophy and medals in the schoolboy association football competition held in the Otley Cricket field on the occasion of the annual demonstration and gala of the Friendly Societies' Association – one of the highlights of the social life of the town in the pre-1914 summers.

Mr. Heppard it was who introduced Soccer into Otley about the end of the last century, and helped to form the first Association Football Club which, in 1898, was renamed Otley Clarence. The headquarters were then at the Woolpack Inn. As the game became more popular, other clubs such as Otley Britannia, White Rose, Victoria, Queen's Hall and Otley Parish Church were formed, and the famous Yorkshire Amateurs played in a field near Otley Mills on Ilkley Road, then owned by Mr. John Mudd, landlord of the Black Bull Inn.

Mr. Loseby, the other teacher, was a Warwickshire man, and a keen cricket follower at a time when the cricket championship was frequently won by his county. He trained some very good schoolboy cricket teams. I still remember, after all this time, a story he used to relate about the Warwickshire player, noted for his prowess as a stumper, who was said to have perfected his ability to catch the ball behind the wicket by going down to the banks of the River Avon and grabbing the swallows as they flew past!

My father was a printer with a small business in Otley, and as my great-grandfather and grandfather had also been in the same trade, my father wanted me to be one too. So, although I had won a County Minor Scholarship to Ilkley Grammar School, I was sent, on the advice of the Headmaster of the North Parade Board School, Mr. Edwin (Gaffer) Smith, to Leeds Boys Modern School "to finish my education" (as the saying was in those days). Mr. Smith was of the opinion that this was the most suitable school at that time for a good grounding in English and Grammar, most necessary in my future trade. Dr. Barber was the Headmaster then. I was there for about two years, and I remember the fees were three guineas per term, plus a charge for text books. The railway pass was £5 per half year. The Modern School at that time was in a building at the end, and adjacent to, the Mechanics' Institute in Cookridge Street in the city. School was on six days a week, but Wednesdays and Saturdays were half-days. Not that the Wednesday half-day was much good for, with the train not reaching Otley until 1 p.m., then dinner to get and homework to do, it was tea-time before a lad was free.

The summer holidays were three weeks, as against the fortnight for elementary schools. Dinners were provided for outside pupils each day at a cost of sixpence, and were served in a dingy basement of the building. And what meals they were! Usually meat and potato pie, with the meat half cooked and the crust as hard as concrete; evil-smelling watery cabbage; and either stiff rice pudding made without sugar and with very little milk, or college pudding – a soggy mess of half-baked dough with a few currants and raisins thrown in, which in later years in the Army I came to know as "plum duff".

It is not surprising that I soon found a better use for that "tanner" by purchasing a couple of big rock buns known as Lockhart's "white elephants", at a penny each from the Cocoa Rooms at the bottom of Briggate, and a penny mug of tea from a stall situated near the first premises of Messrs. Marks and Spencer, Ltd., in the covered market. Twopence admission to the Union Street Swimming Baths nearby, and a penny for the use of a towel accounted for the rest of the sixpence, and I returned to school for the afternoon session suitably refreshed after a delightful swim.

Sometimes I only had one bun, for I was an avid reader of "blood and thunders" in my young days, when one could buy two used copies for a penny at a second hand bookstall in Leeds Market. I still have nostalgic memories of accounts of the lurid adventures of Buffalo Bill in the Wild West; Sexton Blake, the detective; Dick Turpin and Black Bess on their famous ride to York; Claude Duval, another highwayman; Robin Hood and his Merry Men in Green; and Jack, Sam and Pete, a cosmopolitan trio comprised of a White Man, a Negro and an Eskimo, who wandered all over the world.

What is now the Licks Car park, in Otley, just outside the North Parade School, was then the Cattle Market, and sometimes in the summer months travelling theatres with wooden sides and canvas tops, would come for a few weeks with a repertoire of plays and melodramas. These theatres were known as "Threepenny Gaffs", and one of them, I remember, was owned by a man named D'Albert who was quite a character, with a sense of humour, who could appreciate a good joke, even if it was against himself.

On one occasion a "Benefit night" was held in the theatre for the leading lady. The house was crowded and the fun fast and furious. The play presented was "All that Glitters is not Gold",

The Licks car park, formerly a cattle market, about 1904, site of the "threepenny gaffs".

84

and during an interval near the end of the play, Mr. D'Albert addressed the audience thus: "Ladies and gentlemen, I wish to thank you for your good attendance and kind appreication. I would also like to say that I think you are a lot of damned thieves because, although there is a full house, we have taken only five shillings at the pay box. I think the title of the play is most appropriate." It appears that most of the audience had sneaked into the theatre through a hole in the back of the structure, under the gallery seats.

When one of these "Gaffs" departed, we schoolboys used to "scrat" in the cinders outside where the paybox had been, looking hopefully for any silver "threepenny jimmies" that might have dropped. Occasionally we were lucky and found one. That was in the days when potted meat was threepence a half pound at Brown's, the butchers, in Westgate. I can still remember, when we lived in Mount Pisgah, calling there for some after a "windfall", and what an appetising tea I had that day.

After all these years, I still have many recollections of Mount Pisgah,

One such is of the Relief of Mafeking celebrations in the Boer War, when all the youngsters paraded the district wearing various portions of military attire and were photographed by my father. There was a big bonfire in the Market Place on that occasion, the heat of which cracked the windows of shops nearby.

Later on, a crowd of the townspeople, headed by the Otley Band, marched up Burras Lane to "serenade" a man who lived in Clifton Villas, and was reputed to be a pro-Boer. At that time I was, of course, in bed, but I got up, dressed, sneaked out unknown to my parents and followed the crowd. I never got any nearer the house than the railway sidings but in the lulls between the martial music I could hear the sound of stones going through the poor chap's windows. What a terrible thing mob law is. That was my first experience; the second was when I arrived back home and my parents were waiting for me with the strap!

Like many other old terrace houses in the town, those in Mount Pisgah have been modernised and improved, and with

Children of Mount Pisgah celebrating the Relief of Mafeking in 1900.

up-to-date amenities and furnishings are very comfortable, bearing no relation to the Victorian dwellings of those distant years. I lived in one and still have recollections of its austerity, with cellar kitchens, stone floors and steps, the set-pot in the scullery, and no hot water except that heated in the small boiler embodied in the big old-fashioned iron kitchen grate which had to be black-leaded every week; and the out-side "privy", emptied in the small hours by Council workmen, officially desig-nated "night soil workmen", but usually referred to as "midnight mechanics". When, about 1901, and I was ten years of age, my family left to occupy a house in another part of the town which had just previously been built and contained a bathroom, inside toilet and hot and cold water on the sink, it was like living in another world.

Swimming Recollections

I have always loved swimming as a pastime and now, in my eighties, I still enjoy a session in the summer, but in an indoor pool, I must confess. I learned the art at the age of nine in the Goit near Otley Mills in Ilkley Road which, although sometimes swift-running, was not too deep or wide, and a good thrust with the legs sent one across from one bank to the other, with just a flick or two on the way to keep from going under. I think this was the main factor that so quickly gave me the confidence very often lacking in learners, who are afraid that if they go under the water they will never come up again.

In those days, and at that age, we youngsters didn't bother about swimming trunks or such like – just an old pocket handkerchief tied round our middles sufficed! Our parents would have been horrified if they had known what we were up to.

In addition to the Goit, I often swam in the river at the Damstones, near Garnett's Mill, years before Wharfe-meadows Park was made, and there were only fields across which a footpath ran past the "Spring Well", from which flowed the purest water in the district. Occasionally, I also swam in the "Well Holes" just below the filter beds in

The Damstones and Spring Well.

Pool Road, near where there was a deep stretch of the river known as "Fawkes' Deep".

For a change, very often my friends and I would walk to Guiseley, where Mr. Mounsey, a building contractor, had converted a disused Methodist Chapel or Sunday School into a small swimming bath. It was near the old "Drop Inn" and was filled from a spring on Chevin – I think the coldest water I have ever swum in. We soon got warmed up again, however, on our return walk to Otley.

Otley Swimming Club, about 1900.

The spring board

Otley Swimming Club was founded about the beginning of the century, using land and the river near the North side of the Bridge. Starting in a small way, with one little dressing hut, it was at first restricted to male adults. Afterwards boys were admitted as junior members, and in 1904, about the time I joined, the total membership was nearly 200, the number of boys taught to swim being fifty.

In that year, the first annual dinner was held at the Bluebell Inn in Manor Square, a public house long since closed down.

The first president of the Club was Mr. J. M. Wallace, who before coming to reside in Otley, had been a Police Chief Constable in the Shetland Isles; the Secretary was Mr. F. Middleton; and the Treasurer Mr. G. Payne. The Captain was Mr. E. B. Weegman with Mr. C. Bellerby as Vice Captain. Mr. E. Stott had the duties of Instructor and the Committee comprised Messrs. J. Robinson, J. Nicholson, G. Pearson, G. Hobday, S. Stanton, J. Moon, E. Stott, C. Hodgson, E. Hartley, C. Newstead, S. Wallace, R. Stork, A. Rockett, and G. Houlding, practically all being powerful swimmers.

In 1904 the first Water Carnival was held on the river, and it was estimated at the time that 5,000 people were present. In those days, of course, there was no motor traffic and the footway on the east side of the Bridge was not then constructed, so that the bridge was crowded with spectators, some of whom were, even on the buttresses. There was also a big crowd on the south bank, now Manor Park.

The first water carnival prizes in 1904.

Collecting from the crowd on the bridge

Umbrella race across the river

A large number of aquatic events were on the programme, the races being competed for across the river; but the chief item of the afternoon was the high dive from a height of sixty feet by Mr. G. Hobday, who plunged into a pool known locally as "t 'nine oil" — a section of the river judged to be about 15 feet deep.

About this time the name of the Club was changed to "Otley Swimming and Life Saving" and instruction was given in the latter. I gained my bronze medallion in 1913 at Shipley Baths, the Instructor being Mr. Percy Nelson.

The first mixed swimming took place in the river in 1906, and what a sensation it caused. All the people of Otley went along to see the three young ladies from Bradford who had the temerity to swim by the side of men.

I was associated with the Club for ten very happy years until 1914, when I joined the Army. Towards the end of this period I served for some time on the committee and did my "stint" in helping to teach many youngsters to swim. In those days, of course, the fastest stroke was the "trudgeon", used in all races, for the present record-breaking style of relaxed swimming — the "crawl" — had not been introduced.

After heavy rain up the Valley, as so often happens in the autumn, the water of the Wharfe quickly rises, and is soon in spate. One of the most popular practices indulged in when there was just a moderate "fresh" on was to dive into the brown-coloured, peat-tasting flood as it swirled from the end archway of the Bridge, and let it take us in a circular sweep into a little bay just below the springboard, where some of our pals waited to help us out if we overshot the mark. A bit risky, perhaps, but it was worth the thrill — and youth was ever rash!

Mr. G. Hobday diving from a 60 ft. high platform into the river at the carnival.

The first mixed bathers in 1905

A game which demanded a good deal of skill, as well as fast swimming, was a "Duck Hunt". A duck was released into the river and chased until it was caught. At least that was the idea, but it very seldom happened.

Bathing belles

Printing Machine Industry

Although always recognised as a market town — and an important one — Otley has never relied solely on the trade from the surrounding farming community for the prosperity of the bulk of its inhabitants. Other industries have, on occasion, been introduced, one such being the manufacture of printing machines by William Dawson, after the invention of the flat-bed type of press by David Payne about the year 1858, which was later named "The Wharfedale". At a time when the leather trade was declining, these two men by their enterprise and ingenuity ensured the continued prosperity of this town for well over a hundred years, and a belated tribute to their memory is, I venture to say, very much overdue.

A plaque, setting out their achievements, could be erected in a prominent place, where all and sundry could read it, and perhaps be inspired by those immortal lines of the poet, Longfellow: —

> "Lives of great men, all remind us
> We can make our lives sublime,
> And, departing, leave behind us
> Footprints on the sands of time."

There are other worthy men whose names could also be suitably remembered as having helped in the building up of the industry over the years such as the Elliotts, the Watkinsons, the Fieldhouses, the Crossfields, the Kellys and the Stotts; but perhaps the most prominent in later years was Fred Waite, founder of the firm of Waite and Saville Ltd., Falcon Works who, by his inventions, adaptations and improvements (and those of his kinsmen, the Whytes) did his share in creating the printing press as it is today.

Mr. William Dawson

The history of the invention of the "Wharfedale" machine is very interesting. At that time, William Dawson, an Otley joiner of Atlas Works, specialised in the making of sundries for printers and stationers, including a wooden plough and a wooden ruling machine. He was persuaded to construct a new-style, flat-bed printing press, invented by Stephen Soulby of Ulverston in Lancashire, and during its development one of the work–

Mr. David Payne

91

The Ulverston, the first machine made in Otley operated by David Payne and John Fieldhouse.

The second improved machine, with David Payne, Sam Holmes and T.G. Dawson.

men — a man named David Payne whose wages were only one pound a week — suggested many improvements in its design. Work was commenced in 1852 and the machine completed two years later. The principal adopted was that the cylinder travelled over the type, whilst the table remained stationary. The name given to it was "The Ulverston", and for his resource and help, Mr. Soulby presented to David Payne a copy of "The History of Furness Abbey", with a beautiful title page, suitably inscribed.

A second machine made by William Dawson had further modifications made by David Payne, whereby the cylinder travelled half-way, and the table half-way. This was sold to a printer at Lancaster, together with an Otley-made steam engine and boiler, for the sum of £250.

The next machine — constructed in 1858, and named "one of our kind" — was the famous "Wharfedale", in which the table travelled, and the cylinder remained stationary, rotating only — the proper principle. An example can

The flat bed Wharfedale

be seen in the Museum of Otley at the Civic Centre.

Mr. Payne eventually went into partnership with Mr. Dawson at Ashfield Foundry, but afterwards started his own business at Atlas Works, Burras Lane, with his sons. Apparently he had always been of an inventive turn of mind, for he used to relate that he once invented a machine to drain land, which he demonstrated to a farmer in the village in which he then lived. The farmer was so astonished that he swore that if young Payne didn't leave the place he would shoot him, as he was in league with the Devil, otherwise he could not have made a contraption like that!

Ghost Stories

In the past Otley, in common with other small rural places, had its era of superstition and fear of the unknown, when any unusual happening that could not be readily explained was put down to the supernatural.

It was in 1856 that, at one of his lectures, the Rev. Joshua Hart told of the poor old idiot man who, many years before, had been hobbled by the Parish "'cos he run'd away", but who jumped about Cross Green by the aid of a pole. Presumably he was restrained because

he "cast the evil eye". Then there was Molly Topham, whose name is linked with an Otley ghost. Molly's husband was a drunken blacksmith, and she had always to fetch him home from the tavern in the evening. The Barguest, often met Molly and "tried to squeeze her 'gin the wall". The Barguest went on four legs, trailed links of clanking iron, glared and snorted. It was, of course, one of the large mastiffs kept by the Parish Constable to enforce law and order when the local Poorhouse and Lockup were in Cross Green.

The bone house shown near the Church tower

Up to about 1890 there was a Bone House in the recess on the north side of the Parish Church, near the Tower, where bones disinterred in the Churchyard were thrown. A story is told of two men who, drinking in the Black Bull Inn many years ago, got boasting of their courage, and one bet the other a gallon of ale that he dare not go at midnight and fetch a skull from the Bone House. This challenge was accepted and in due course the man set off to win his bet.

The other, slipping out another way, hurried up and hid in a corner of the Bone House, and when the boaster came in and got hold of a skull, he said in a sepulchral voice, "That's mine," and so it was thrown down, and when another was picked up and the voice said, "That's my father's," that also was discarded. But after hearing, "That's my grandfather's," on picking up the third, the now thoroughly frightened man exclaimed, "Who art tha'?" "I'm the Devil," came the reply. "Well, I think tha's a very greedy Devil," said he and, grabbing another skull, rushed to the Black Bull where he threw it on the floor shouting, "I've won, but it's the Devil's, and he's coming for it!"

About a hundred years ago — in 1870 — my grandfather, James Walker, commenced business as a printer in a building in Market Place, Otley, near the Jubilee Clock. Here he also lived and, incidentally, I was born there. My grandfather had previously worked as a journeyman for Messrs. Webb, Millington & Co. (afterwards the Yorkshire Joint Stock Publishing Company, Ltd.) in their premises opposite the Maypole,

Mr. James Walker, on his home made tricycle

94

Mrs. Horner, the "planet ruler"

if he was not working he would doze before the fire.

One morning, in the small hours, he was making his way to bed and had climbed two flights of stairs when, to his amazement, he saw an old woman in a frilled cap, with a candle in her hand, come down from one of the top rooms. He turned tail, ran back into the kitchen, where he got a light, and ever after no one could induce him to go to bed without one.

His description of the apparition was that of old Mrs. Horner who, for 60 years, had lived in that house until her death, mother of Mr. James Horner, the first Secretary of the Mechanics' Institute. She was a "planet ruler", and there was a story that when one day she broke an egg, out rolled a sixpence, and after that her family's luck changed for the better and they prospered exceedingly.

but he thought he could do better on his own account. He was what I have heard described as a "good worker in the morning the night before", as he seldom went to bed before 1 a.m., and

In these modern times most of us claim not to be superstitious. I know I'm not, but I never walk under ladders, and if I spill any salt I always throw a pinch over my left shoulder! I wonder why?

Early Days on Wheels

A Trans-Pennine Rally of ancient commercial motor vehicles reminded me of the first motor car to be driven through the streets of Otley. It was, I think, on a Rally from London to Edinburgh in 1900 — a wonderful feat to attempt in those early motor pioneering days — and was photographed at the top of Boroughgate, before the car rounded the Black Horse Hotel corner. The road was then paved with cobblestones. The picture also shows the first policeman on "point duty" directing the

The first motor car through the town

traffic. I would be about nine years old at the time, and a pupil at the North Parade Board School. I well remember we children being let out of school to see the wonderful "horseless carriage". This car was, I think, an open two-seater De Dion with a dickey seat. There was no hood or covering against the weather, and no windscreen.

W.H. Dawson was the first Otley resident to own a car

The first motor car in the Otley district was, to my recollection, owned by Mr. William Henry Dawson of Maple Bank (now known as Maple Grange) just off the Burley Road, about 1903, who died of pneumonia in 1905 at the early age of 42. He was an officer in the Otley Company of the Second West Yorkshire Royal Engineers Volunteers, which was based in Leeds, and I still have vivid memories of the military funeral to Otley Cemetery, the most impressive event of its kind ever seen in the town up to then.

Other early cars of the period were owned by Mr. Fred Waite, founder of the firm of Waite and Saville Ltd., printers' engineers, Otley; and Mr. Henry Dacre,

who built the Recreation Hall in Church Lane.

In later years, after the invention of the "White" steam car, Messrs. David Payne and Sons, who were local agents, built premises at the bottom of Well Hill, Westgate, to accommodate the models. I think Col. W. C. Dawson, of Weston Hall, acquired one; also Mrs. Constable of the Manor House, Otley, whose chauffeur was Mr. Charles A. Sellers. Messrs. Payne's first demonstrator and salesman for the steam car was Mr. Robert Slater, whose wife was the daughter of Mr. Senior Blackburn, a former well-known Otley pork butcher and pie maker, who for many years lived at Jenny's Cottage on Chevin Top. As a private chauffeur to Mr. Fred Payne, Mr. Slater subsequently drove one of the steam cars for several years after Payne and Sons discontinued handling them commercially.

Mr. Denny Waite lived and kept a small sweet shop in Kirkgate, where the Church wall now is. He was also a horse-cab and wagonette proprietor, who eventually went into the taxi hire business in the early days of the present century, using Ford "Model T" cars. Mr. Frank Abram was one of his drivers for many years, and also Mr. Baden Powell Green.

Another pioneer taxi firm which used Ford "Model T" cars, was R. Richardson and Sons, who were also grocers and cab proprietors at the corner of Kirkgate and Bondgate. The late Mr. D'Arcy Richardson will still be remembered as the prime mover on the taxi side. It is interesting to note that for many years, before the construction of the branch railway line from Arthington to Ilkley, Mr. Robert Richardson carried the Royal Mail morning and evening between Arthington and Otley and was, in fact, the last stage coach proprietor in the district on the route from Arthington that had been travelled by my father when, as an infant in 1863, he came with his family from Sheffield to settle in Otley.

Mr. Payne's White Steam car, driven by Bob Slater

Richardson's premises at the corner of Kirkgate and Bondgate

Brass Bands of the Past

Otley Engineers Volunteers band, 1876.

In past years Otley was noted for the excellence of its Brass Bands, and in my youth one or another of them was a social amenity of the town.

Many years ago the old Toll Bar House at the top of Bridge Street, demolished in 1928, was the practice place for the local Brass Band, and the conductor for a time was David Payne who, besides being an inventor, was also a talented cornettist. He also had a sense of humour, as shown by the following anecdote he used to relate.

What we know now as Courthouse Street was then Back Lane, the name only being changed after the Courthouse and police offices were built in 1874, and at the end where is now a chemists' shop — just round the corner from where the bar house stood — was a small "one up and one down" house tenanted by an old lady who loved the weekly practice nights of the band. On one occasion when they were belting out one of the overtures then popular, she could contain her enthusiasm no longer, but rushed round to the band premises, where she banged on the door shouting, "Ee lads, ye're playing better n'ivver ta neet, so all on ye come ahtside an' listen ta yersels."

In the summer of 1878 Wm. Christopher Dawson, Esq., of Weston Hall, became 21 years of age. He was then captain in charge of the Otley Company of the 2nd West Yorkshire Royal Engineers Volunteers, based in

Colonel W. C. Dawson

98

Leeds, the whole unit of which mustered round about 1,000 men. To mark the occasion, the unit had a "Field Day" in Weston Park. This included marching, rifle-firing, refreshments and dancing to the Otley Company Band, whose instruments had been bought and loaned to the band by Mrs. Dawson, the Captain's mother.

In the same year two grand performances were given on Redcar pier by this band, under the able leadership of Mr. Fred Bell, and the splendid new instruments attracted much attention.

Mr. Fred Bell

The pier was crowded on both occasions. The expenses of the trip were paid by Mrs. Dawson, who also subsequently defrayed the cost of a lifeboat at Redcar. A stained glass window depicting the lifeboat, commemorating the gift, from the people of Redcar, can be seen in Weston Parish Church.

Mr. Bell was, in his later years, the musical director of the Scarborough Municipal Orchestra which played on the Spa. He was the son-in-law of Mr. G. D. Wigglesworth who, over a hundred years ago, made musical instruments in his workshop in Newmarket. Mr. Wigglesworth was the great grandfather of the

G.D. Wigglesworth with an ophicleide

wife of my late brother Jimmy. She was a member of the Suttle family, and they had in their possession a cornet and clarinet made by Mr. Wigglesworth, and now in their daughter's possession.

I think there are still one or two specimens of Mr. Wigglesworth's work in private hands in the town, but none in the local museum, although an instrument he made — known as an ophicleide — a French invention which superseded the serpent, is in Keighley Museum.

Col. W. C. Dawson eventually commanded the whole 2nd West Yorkshire Volunteers, from 1887 to 1903, but with his resignation the Otley-formed band broke up and the Dawson family repossessed the instruments.

Col. Dawson's Otley band

Shortly afterwards, however, a private band was formed known as Col. Dawson's (Otley) Band, which used the same instruments, and they were also provided with smart new uniforms, black with white facings, by the Colonel. The conductor was Mr. T. P. Newton, a well-known local musician, who had succeeded his brother-in-law (Mr. Charlie Bolton) as the leader of the Engineers Band. At one time he was licensee of the Fountain Hotel, Otley.

The Band was often in demand for such functions as garden parties, dances, the annual Whit Monday walk of the Nonconformist Sunday School scholars, and the yearly demonstration and gala of the Local Friendly Societies' Association which concluded with dancing and fireworks in the cricket field, and was reckoned to be the best of the season's events.

With the formation of Lord Haldane's Territorial Army in 1907, the members of Col. Dawson's Band were recruited en bloc into the 4th West Riding Howitzer Brigade, R.F.A., as the Brigade Band with Headquarters at Bradford. For several years, until the commencement of the 1914-18 war, when it "stood down", the Band participated in the social activities of the district, and was sadly missed for a long time. The instruments were eventually purchased by the Territorial Army Association.

After the war, when the Howitzer Brigade, R.F.A., was reconstructed with headquarters again at Bradford, the Band was reformed and accompanied the Brigade to the first post-war camp at Scarborough under the conductorship of Mr. J. Curtis.

The Rev. Arthur Baldwin

When the Otley Local Board of Health — the forerunner of the Urban District Council — was formed in 1864, Mr. William Baldwin, an Otley Man, became the first Surveyor at a wage of 24/- per week, which was increased to 5/- a day after seven years' service.

Mr. Baldwin's father, John, was the first person to be interred in the new cemetery opened in the year 1862 by the Otley, Lindley and Newall-with-Clifton Joint Burial Board. He was a noted character known, for some reason or other, as "Old Jacky Beanland", and had a reputation locally as a healer of "demic" and boils. It used to be

Rev. Arthur Baldwin

humorously said that "Jacky" was not the first to be buried in the Cemetery, for he was only part of a man, having previously lost a leg, which was in the Parish Churchyard!

The Rev. Arthur Baldwin — the son of William and the grandson of John — was born in Otley, entered the Primitive Methodist Ministry and at one part of his career was in charge of the Otley Station Road Chapel.

He led an eventful life. In 1889 he left England as one of a party for missionary work in Africa, eventually reaching country north of the Zambesi River, a region never previously penetrated by white folk. It is now a part of Rhodesia and Mr. Eric Girling former Surveyor of Otley Urban District Council, who was born in Rhodesia, brought to my notice the fact that the Rev. Arthur Baldwin was the man who first drew to the attenion of pros— pectors the presence of the vast deposits of copper in that region.

Mr. Girling also kindly gave me a copy of an article published in "The Northern Rhodesia Journal" in 1952, written by the Rev. J. R. Shaw, which makes interesting reading, telling the story of two men and one woman who set off from Kimberley in 1890, in three tent-covered springless wagons, each pulled by 18 oxen, and a Scotch cart with six oxen, to establish a Mission Station at Nkala (now at Namwala) on the Kafue River, a trek which took three years and nine months.

The hardships they endured on the way are well-nigh unbelievable. The Zambesi River was reached where it is almost a thousand yards wide, and the wagons had to be taken to pieces and floated over. The oxen swam over, one by one, and the goods were transported in dug-out canoes. In all, 17 rivers and river beds had to be crossed, one of them five times. Three bridges had to be built strong. enough to carry a wagon. A

101

wagon wheel hit a stump and every spoke was broken. The travellers had to make a new wheel before they could proceed. The making of a new nave for the wheel took ten days.

In December 1893, the wagons emerged from the bush to the edge of the Kafue plains, but it was the wet season, and no time for building. Simple huts were erected, and the party held on amidst rain, flood, fever and dysentry, and undisciplined savages. The year of their arrival was the year of the occupation of Matabeleland to the south.

With regard to the discovery of copper, let me quote what the Rev. J. R. Shaw says in his article. He writes: "One day a long line of porters and three white prospectors appeared on the Plain making for the Mission Station at Nkala. These men were from Matabeleland, and had naturally made for the dwelling of the only white residents in the whole country. They were welcomed and entertained. The missionaries had done a great deal of local travelling and so these prospectors enquired if they had seen any signs of minerals. Looking from Nkala to the north are the Kafue Plains and then a long line of hills. The Rev. Baldwin told of his trekking through that distant area. There he had noticed the people were wearing copper rings and anklets. He had brought back a few stones which appeared to show signs of minerals.

The prospectors promptly recognised copper in the stones and gladly accepted them from Mr. Baldwin. Two of the men went north to locate and peg the mineral discovery and the third returned at once south to the Zambesi and to Matabeleland with the samples of the find of copper. He sold the rights to develop these claims — which he had never seen himself — to one of the new mining companies for several thousand pounds. Then the Northern Copper Company was formed and the Sable Mine in the Mumbwa District was opened. It was from that Sable Mine that other men went further north and saw the signs which led to the development of the present copperbelt. The finder of the first modern copper deposit was thus the Rev. Arthur Baldwin.

The date the missionaries entered Northern Rhodesia should be noted. It was the year 1890, i.e. before Southern Rhodesia was occupied. Also it was a long time before there was any government, law or police north of the Zambesi River.

Arthur Baldwin was one of those quiet, faithful, brave men who seek no notoriety and no wealth from their service of God and Man, concludes the writer.

Military Men

Down the ages, when occasion arose, Otley produced its fighting men, from the days of the Picts and Scots, and it is on record that Otley men fought at the Battle of Marston Moor.

At the time of the Boer War (1899-1902) I should be eight or nine years of age, and remember that a Company of the Wharfedale Yeomanry was raised by Capt. Lane-Fox, of Bramham Hall. Amongst them were many Otley men, and training was done in the grounds of the Manor House, Otley, before embarkation for active service in South Africa. There were also many volunteers from the Otley Company of the Royal Engineers Volunteers — the "Saturday

Trooper John Wilton Sedman

Otley Company — Wharfedale Yeomanry

103

Night Soldiers" as they were jocularly referred to in those days — in addition to Otley men who, as Army reservists, were "called up" for service. The names of two Otley men who lost their lives in the Transvaal are recorded on a tablet affixed to the Jubilee Clock. One was Trooper John Wilton Sedman, whose war medal and clasps, awarded posthumously, were given to me by his sister, the late Miss Annie Sedman. I have since handed them over to the Museum of Otley, for preservation. The other name on the tablet is that of Sapper Vantress Duell, aged 20, of the Royal Engineers Volunteers. Both were buried in South Africa. Sgt. Charles Humphreys of the Royal Engineers Volunteers, who served in the Boer War, afterwards became one of the first Labour Councillors to serve on Otley Urban District Council. Private John Devanney, of the Black Watch (The Royal Highlanders) was wounded at the storming of Spion Kop.

In the 1914-18 war, over 500 Otley men joined the various branches of the forces. Many were killed, and their names appear on the War Memorial Cross in the Garden of Remembrance in Bondgate. Some were decorated for gallantry and distinguished service. At that time the Territorial Army had come

Sgt. Charles Humphreys

Town celebrations at the Relief of Mafeking

10th Howitzer battery

The battery in Leeds Road, August 1914

Siege of Mafeking one pound note

into force, the 10th Battery of the 4th West Riding Howitzer Brigade, Royal Field Artillery being the local unit. Although raised for home defence only, the Howitzer Battery, like the rest of the Territorial Army, volunteered for overseas service and served abroad from 1915, with distinction, taking part in many engagements in France and Belgium. In 1939-46 the Howitzer Battery served in many theatres of war, and the names of those killed together with those of the men who lost their lives in other Corps. and regiments are recorded on a plaque in the Garden of Remembrance. Older men in the town and those in reserved occupations served in the local Home Guard Unit, and I have recorded their activities elsewhere in this book.

The full brigade leaving for France, June 1915

A Home-coming of Years Ago

Most people getting on in years will agree with me that some memories of our past lives stand out more vividly in our minds than others, and these are usually the more enjoyable ones. As the most momentous and happiest thing that ever happened to me was demobilization from the Army, in the February of 1919, after the conclusion of hostilities in the first world-war, perhaps I may be pardoned for recalling it.

The author on overseas service

At the time of the Armistice in November, 1918, I was in Italy, serving in a Field Ambulance with the Seventh Division, which had been sent there, along with the 23rd and 48th, after the surrender of the Italian Army under General Cadorna to the Germans and Austrians in the Autumn of 1917. I think the idea was to boost the morale of the Italian public, which had fallen very low after the collapse of their Army, but the brunt of the subsequent fighting fell on these three British Divisions. I had a pretty rough time in the Piave River Crossing and Asiago Plateau operations and had to be sent down to Base with Disorderly Action of the Heart (D.A.H.) and Debility, being marked "B2".

I was in the 11th General Hospital at Genoa when the Armistice was signed, and not very long after was sent to a Dispersal Camp preparatory to the journey back to "Blighty" for demobilisation. I still have vivid memories of that Camp at Aquatta. The weather in Northern Italy was pretty atrocious in the months of December and January with its almost continuous rain, sleet and snow, and the only consolation was that we had tents in which to sleep, in contrast to the lads in the "line", even if the water did flow in a stream through them, and we were never dry.

Anyway we moved eventually, and after a nightmare journey of three weeks across France in cattle trucks via the Mont Cenis Tunnel through the Alps, and living on Machonocie stew, biscuits and "bully", we arrived at Dieppe, thence across the water to Southampton and "Merrie England" — though not so merry as we could have liked it at that period of the year, for when we arrived at Clipston Camp at about 11 p.m. on a Saturday night, after just a sandwich and pot of tea for sustenance all day, it was freezing and the subsequent medical examination in a cold hutment was not very popular!

The following morning (Sunday) I managed to get to Leeds by train, but as the local service to Otley was off, I got a tram to the White Cross, Guiseley. Unfortunately for me the trackless tram service from there to Otley also did not start until the afternoon, and in my worn-out uniform and carrying my meagre possessions in a sandbag, I started on the four miles to the "Metropolis of Wharfedale". I just couldn't make it, and fell out at the Fox and Hounds Hotel, Menston. The Landlord telephoned for a taxi and so I arrived home, where my wife greeted me with, "Dinner won't be long, love; the Yorkshire pudding is in the oven. I knew you were coming." Now that was a queer thing for her to say for, after not hearing from me for several weeks she could not have known that I was on my way home − and it brings me to the gist of my narrative.

It seems that my wife had gone on a visit to her father at Yeadon on the Saturday. Next door to him lived Mrs. Annie Blackburn, who had something of a reputation as a fortune teller and reader of cards. Seeing my wife in the garden, shortly after her arrival, Mrs. Blackburn asked how long she was staying. On being told she was there for the week-end, she strongly advised her to go back to Otley as soon as possible, as I was on my way home. This my wife did, in spite of her father's efforts to dissuade her, and that is why I sat down to the best Sunday dinner I ever enjoyed in my life. It is also why I never scoff at so-called fortune telling, as I firmly believe that some people do have the gift of seeing into the future.

The Home Guard

These memories − humorous and otherwise − of Britain's wartime civilian Army, which was composed of men who were too old or unfit for the Forces, or were in reserved occupations, will perhaps prove entertaining.

Otley Company, Home Guard, Burras Lane, 1942

It was in May, 1940, after Dunkirk and Sir Winston Churchill's famous "fighting on the beaches" speech, that Sir Anthony Eden made his appeal for volunteers to a local defence force to help repel any threatened invasion. Known at first as the Local Defence Volunteers ("L.D.V.") – the name was afterwards changed to the Home Guard and became a part-time military organisation under the control of the Territorial Association.

Affiliated to the West Riding Regiment, the 29th (Otley) Battalion included places such as Ilkley, Baildon, Pool and the surrounding rural districts, Otley itself being "A" Company. The Headquarters Company of the Battalion was also stationed in the town.

History was repeating itself, as it so often does, for early in the nineteenth century, when Napoleon and his Army were assembled near Calais for a contemplated invasion of England, the Rev. James Bailey, Vicar of Otley, a member of the Shaw family who lived in Boroughgate; and Mr. Clifton Wilkinson, of Newall Hall (who later became its Commandant)formed "The Otley Armed Band Association", the drum of which, embellished with the Coat of Arms, is now in the Museum of Otley.

"A" Company of the Home Guard was stationed at the Drill Hall, where many ex-Servicemen, including myself, enrolled, and the place was soon the busiest building in the town, with the warlike activities that went on each evenings and at week-ends. I never ceased to wonder how a building, commencing its existence as a House of God could, over the years, become a Temple of Mars; and what the Rev. John Wesley, who had preached the opening sermon in 1772 when it became a Wesleyan meeting-house, would have thought had he been alive!

To "A" Company had been given the task of guarding the pipe lines at the Leeds City Council's reservoirs at Fewston, Swinsty and Lindley, from any sabotage that might be attempted, and each night a party of twenty men, in the charge of a Sergeant, was taken out to the Washburn Valley for that purpose. The Otley party went to Fewston and Swinsty, and the Lindley reservoir was the responsibility of the Pool detachment.

In the early days when the weather was fairly warm, the men were conveyed on open lorries, but as time went on buses were made available. They usually left about 8.30 p.m. returning at 5.30 the next morning. I remember on one occasion that when a bus broke down at the top of Carr Bank, the men were in the "Spite" like a flash, all intent on "doing in" their subsistence allowance of three bob each, on liquid refreshment. It took all my powers of cajolory to get them out when the replacement vehicle turned up, and I had visions of having to do the guard myself. Unlike a regular, an N.C.O. in the Home Guard couldn't "pull rank" – he would soon have been told where to go had he tried it.

In the early days the guard party had a mixed collection of weapons, from muzzle loaders to .22 Winchesters and shot guns, and these had to be fetched and returned to the Police Station each day, where they were locked in a cell for safety. Later, when things became more organised, American rifles made in 1917, and used by their troops in France in the 1914-18 war, which had been in storage in America for nearly twenty years, were issued. Known as the "P.17" (pattern of 1917), they were long, heavy rifles, of .300 calibre, as against the short Lee Enfield .303 used by the British in the 1914-18 war and the first four years of the last conflict. The "P.17" was very accurate though, particularly at 300 yards, and some of the members of the Home Guard became very expert in its use.

There were two guard posts at the reservoirs – one in an outhouse at the engineer's residence near the embankment at Fewston; and the other at the caretaker's house at Swinsty where the guard commander and the larger number of the party stayed. The two posts were connected by telephone. There were various points where sentries were stationed, and the period of duty for each man was two hours.

Apart from a little egg pinching, and the surrepticious milking of a cow or two in the early morning by young and irresponsible members, I realize how lucky it was that nothing serious happened during the four years or so the Home Guard was at the reservoirs.

The only thing that really shook me, also had its funny side. The firm order was that when a sentry came off duty he unloaded his rifle before entering the Guardroom, which at Swinsty was the residence of Mr. John Dunn, the caretaker. On one occasion a member of my party came into the Guardroom and, in reply to my query, said he had unloaded his magazine. As I turned away there was a sudden flash and explosion which blew out the hurricane oil lamp we had for illumination, and a bullet ploughed into the ceiling above, bringing down a length of plaster. He must have had a round "up the spout" when he unloaded, which he had forgotten about. Anyway, after a few minutes the inside door of the guardroom burst open, and Mr. Dunn, clad only in his shirt, and with bare feet, rushed in, and the language he used is unprintable. It appears he had been sleeping in the bedroom above and only the linoleum on the floor had prevented the bullet from bursting through.

The guarding of the reservoirs was only incidental to the training that took place almost every evening, in arms drill, lectures and tactics, with out-of-doors operations at the weekends that invariably provided something out of the ordinary. We once had an exercise at Arthington, where enemy troops were supposed to be trying to demolish the viaduct. After a forced march from Otley, we came in sight of our objective and chased across fields to dislodge the saboteurs. Unfortunately, Mr. Ernest Stewart and I got into a field belonging to Mr. Benny Mills, in which there was a bull that spotted us before we saw it. Getting its head down, and with its tail up, it chased after us, and I don't think two middle-aged men had ever run faster We beat the beast to the hedge by a short head, only to fall into a beck on the other side! We both had a wet march home.

Other episodes were the all-night exercises in all sorts of weather — mostly bad — when we "dossed down" in barns and outhouses in outlying farms, and the only good things were the hot meals of sausage and mash prepared by the ladies of the Canteen at the Drill Hall and sent out to us in insulated containers. The Canteen facilities, by the way, were exceptionally good. Situated in one of the upper rooms of the Drill Hall, refreshments were available each evening and at weekends. The service was originally inaugurated by the W.V.S. in charge of Mrs. Cyril Banks, but after a time was taken over by my wife, Lillian, Mrs. Norah Hall and Mrs. Kathleen Whitaker, who were enrolled as "Women Home Guard Auxiliaries", of whom there were only five in Otley. The other two were Mrs. Cyril Banks; and Mrs. Jack Batty, of the clerical staff.

An asset the Otley company possessed for a time was the Drum and Fife Band, jocularly referred to as the "spit and whistle". Trained by Mr. H. J. Laker and Mr. Reg Rawling, the number of tunes was naturally limited, but they certainly did make the route marches more enjoyable. Indeed "Blaydon Races" was played with so much gusto that the Geordie evacuees in the town wept "buckets-full" when they heard it. Unfortunately, the Band was composed of the younger element, who were "called up" in the regular forces in

Col. Duncan taking the Battalion stand down salute

turn, and so it finally ceased to exist. I believe the Messenger Corps eventually got the instruments.

During my service with the Home Guard, I attended the West Riding Weapons Training School at Harlow Grange, Harrogate, for a week-end course in grenades, in order to "pass out" as an instructor. Most of the time was taken up by theoretical talks preparatory to the practical work on the Sunday afternoon, which finished off the course and included the live throwing of grenades. Before being allowed to take the tests, however, each pupil on the grenade course had to throw a "dud" grenade over a wire stretched between two tall trees in the grounds adjoining the house. Failure to do so, we were told by the instructor, a regular Army sergeant, meant that we would not be allowed to throw "live". The instructor took us alone, one by one, to the wire, but when my turn came, could I heck as get the thing over; it was too much for my puny strength. However when, after several futile attempts, the fellow casually asked me if I could throw a "dollar" over, I "tumbled", and handed five bob to him. Damn me, I thought, the Army's still the same as it was when I was in all those years before. That chap must have been augmenting his pay by several pounds a week. Well, I "passed out", and came away with my certificate.

All things come to an end, and at the Battalion "stand-down" parade at Ilkley, in December 1944, the Commanding Officer, Col. Hugh S. Duncan, M.C.,T.D., thanked all ranks for their services, and afterwards took the salute in The Grove, at the March Past.

Contrary to what the present generation has been led to believe, at the time of its disbandment the Home Guard was an efficient body of men, highly trained in the use of weapons of all kinds — of which there were plenty — who would have given a good account of themselves in any contingency.

It must not be forgotten also, that the invasion army which landed in Normandy when the "second front" was opened, contained a high proportion of soldiers who had served in the Home Guard before being "called up", and the knowledge they had acquired there not only lessened the period of their training, but heightened their efficiency as regular soldiers.

110

The Statute Hirings

Potential farm labourers for the Statute Hirings

In past years, November was the traditional month for the annual Statute Hirings at Martinmas, held on the Fridays before and after the 23rd, but now, like many other customs, with changing habits they are no longer celebrated. Then it was that a farmer seeking a good "hand", or a man after a fresh job and a new employer, met in the Market Place at Otley, and agreed on terms for the coming year's work. To seal the transaction, the farm-hand received a "God's Penny", and this also applied to girls and women recruited for farm service in the same way.

In 1882, the following prices were asked and given; all round men from £25 to £30 for the year; second class men £18 to £25; strong youths £14 to £16; boys from £10 to £14; females of experience £18 to £30; younger ones £15; girls £8 to £10. These wages included board and lodging in addition.

With the coming of Labour Exchanges, there was a noticeable decrease each year in the amount of business done in Otley Market Place, and wages were not so high as previously. In 1912, all-round men from 23 to 25 years of age commanded £20 to £24; and second-class men got £14 to £17. In 1916, when the first World War was at its height, owing to conscription in the Forces there was naturally a shortage of men, and the only labour available was that of a few boys who demanded £15 to £20, according to experience. Not very long after, the custom was abandoned entirely.

As the lads and lasses had received a year's wages from previous employers, there was always plenty of money about at "Stattis" as it was called locally and, as is customary at such times, lots of people ready to relieve them of it. The fairground attractions, if anything more numerous than at Feast-time, and extended over two week-ends, called to the youth of the district, and if funds were too low — well, one could always purchase "a ha'porth o'peas, an' can I laik wi' t'monkey please?" Local tradespeople also benefitted exceedingly by the replenishment of wearing apparel and other necessary items.

Concerning Rugby Football

I have been associated with many of the social activities and institutions of Otley during my lifetime, perhaps the most enjoyable of these being my connection of over twenty-five years with Otley Rugby Union Football Club, both as a player and an official. "Rugger" has been popular in the town for almost a hundred years and, in fact, an Otley Rugby team won the Yorkshire Challenge Cup Competition in 1889 by beating Liversedge at Cardigan Fields, Leeds.

Victors over Liversedge

The score was the close one of four points to three in Otley's favour and the Captain was Mr. Fred Mudd. The President of the Club at that time was Mr. H. W. T. Garnett, head of the Wharfeside Paper Mills at Otley.

In the year 1900, owing to certain grievances against the Yorkshire County Committee, the Otley Club turned over to professional football, and joined the newly-formed Northern Union — now the Rugby League. They were not very successful, however, and it was decided in 1904 to disband and sell the property held by the Committee. However, in 1907, the brothers Harold and Kenneth, sons of Mr. Thomas Arthur Duncan, of Westbourne House, Otley, with other interested parties, re-formed the Otley Club to again play the amateur code. They were recognised by the County Committee; Mr. H. W. T. Garnett again became the President, shortly afterwards followed by Mr. Harry Barker, of Torrocks Hill, Pool, and the matches once

The revived team, and cup winners, in 1910

more were played on the Wharfeside ground.

As a youth of sixteen, I took a fancy to the game, and went pretty regularly to Wharfeside on practice nights. The headquarters were at the Queen's Head Hotel in Kirkgate, closed down many years ago, and the dressing rooms in a disused stable, up a ramp, at the rear of the public house. On match days, players had to clump across the Market Place, down the Bay Horse Passage, and through the Licks, on the way to the ground, in their heavily-studded football boots and togs. One or two players I have known in the past to slip into the Bay Horse — there was then a side door in the passage — to "wet their whistles" on the way.

There was only one big bath tub in the Dressing Rooms, and this would hold several players at a time. It was high and square, made of wood lined with zinc, which was filled with boiling hot water by a chap named Sandy Stewart, who brought it up in buckets from the kitchen of the pub. After a match, players had to run like the devil if they wished to bathe in clean water, for the Wharfeside ground was always waterlogged in one place or another, and was notorious as the muckiest in the county. Late arrivals usually had to bathe in liquid mud!

I was never much more than an average player — a stalwart of the second team, one might say — but sometimes I got a game with the senior side, and in the 1913-14 season did so fourteen or fifteen times, mostly at "away" matches, but also quite a few at Wharfeside. I had good hopes of a permanent place the following season, but Kaiser Bill put a stop to that, and I was in the Army for the next four and a half years. I only played once after demobilization, in 1919, at Skipton in the first match of the

1928 – 29 Cup winners

113

season, when I realized that, at the age of 27, the game of rugby was too hard for an "ex-swaddy", and so "I packed it in".

About sixty playing members of the Otley Rugby Club joined the forces in the first world war – I don't know how many did so in the 1939-46 upheaval – and they didn't all come back. Douglas Elliott, Frank Hymas, Vivian Kidd, Albert Lockwood, W. Preston, Harold Stephenson, Harry Todd and Arthur Wise all made the supreme sacrifice, and Norman Barker, Tom Brotherton, George Crow, Kenneth Duncan, Hugh S. Duncan, W. Othic and Arthur Wise received honours or decorations, a wonderful record for a small town Club.

My career as an official commenced in the 1920-21 season, when I was appointed Hon. Assistant to Mr. Frank E. Whyte, and until the 1935-6 season, when I reluctantly had to resign owing to the illness of my father, with whom I was in business, I was in turn Team, Fixture, Joint and General Secretary.

Play on the Wharfeside ground became increasingly difficult so, mainly through the efforts of Messrs. Fred Waite, William H. Barker and Phil S. Wade, the present ground at Cross Green was bought.

One of the last games to be played on the Wharfeside ground was in 1921, when an "In Memoriam" match to Yorkshire rugby players who had lost their lives in the War, between a Yorkshire team and one from Wharfedale, resulted in a win for Yorkshire by 23 points to 3. There were eight players from Otley and seven from Ilkley in the Wharfedale side.

Otley has won the final of the Yorkshire Challenge Cup competition seven times since 1889, the most memorable one, as far as I am concerned, being in the 1928-29 season. On that occasion the President, Mr. Fred Waite, presented a solid silver cigarette case to each of the players and officials at a dinner he gave at the "Black Horse" Hotel, to which he invited players, officials, committee and ladies' committee.

Old Salem Chapel

The Salem Chapel, demolished towards the end of the nineteenth century, stood on the site of the present Bridge Church in Bridge Street. Opened in 1826, it was a dour building, standing as forthright as those sturdy "Independents" who were the first Nonconformists to break away from the orthodox church in order to indulge in a simpler form of worship.

Old Salem Chapel from the bridge

Collapse of the scaffolding

whilst two of the stone masons were on the scaffold building the wall above the North window, a stone gave way and a large part of the wall collapsed on to the scaffold, bringing it down. The men fell 40 feet, and one of them – Mr. Benjamin Bateson, of Burley-in-Wharfedale, was killed. Mr. Flesher, of Otley, the other man, was badly injured.

Public sympathy was aroused for Mr. Bateson's widow and five children, and collections were taken in the town to help them. A travelling theatre which happened to be in the Licks, named "The Alhambra", owned by Mr. G. W. Vickers, gave a benefit performance in aid of the fund.

The Sunday School premises were opened in 1882, and during construction,

Passing of the Toll Bar Houses

In former years Otley, like many other townships, had its Toll Bar Houses, to collect revenue for the upkeep of the turnpike roads. These houses were sited at the top of Bridge Street (then known as Northgate); the bottom of East Chevin, near the Fountain Inn; just above the Cemetery in Pool Road;

Toll Bar house in Bridge Street, demolished in 1928

115

Toll Bar house at the junction of West Chevin Road and Bradford Road, demolished in the 1930's.

near the entrance to Grove Hill Park in Ilkley Road; and the bottom of West Chevin Road at its junction with Bradford Road. Tolls ceased to be collected in 1874, and since that time, all the Bar Houses have been pulled down, with the exception of one — that at the bottom of East Chevin Road in Gay Lane, which is now a lock-up retail shop. Built in 1850, it was here that Lady Snowdon, wife of the Labour Cabinet Minister, Lord Snowdon, lived with her aunt before she married Philip Snowdon at the Otley Register Office in Boroughgate.

This interesting photograph depicts the then Duke of Devonshire passing the toll bar house in a carriage and horses, with outriders, as he drove up Gay Lane to Otley Railway Station, after officially opening the Unionist Club in Boroughgate, in 1893.

The Duke of Devonshire passing the Toll Bar house in Gay Lane

The Jubilee Clock

One of the attractive features of the centre of Otley is the Jubilee Clock, built to commemorate the Golden Jubilee of Her Majesty Queen Victoria, in 1887. It was officially started by Master Harold Duncan, elder son of Mr. Thomas Arthur Duncan, of Westbourne, Otley, Chairman of the Local Board of Health. Mr. James Johnson, on behalf of the Committee which planned the memorial, presented the tower, clock, drinking fountain, and seats to the Local Board, in trust for the people of the town.

Both Mr. Duncan and Mr. Johnson were members of the Jubilee Committee, which also included Messrs. Thomas Buck, E. Bullivant, William C. Weegman, Albert Walker, Alfred Marshall and J. E. Towney.

In addition to the plaque to the memory of the two Otley men who lost their lives in the Boer War, there is also one recording the thanks of the Belgian refugees to the people of Otley for their hospitality during the war of 1914-18.

The Jubilee Clock

Town Cryers

Otley has never possessed a Town Cryer, or Bellman, as they were called, since 1915 when the last person to hold that office died. He was Mr. Thomas Mann — familiarly known as Tommy Mann — a respected member of the Salvation Army community in the town, who lived at one time in a house in one of the yards off Kirkgate. Previous Bellmen were Mr. Cawood, and Mr. Isaac Pollard, who was also the local Bill Poster.

Thomas Mann, the last town crier

117

Mr. Cawood

Isaac Pollard

The Navvy's Friend

The daughter of the Rev. Joshua Hart, Vicar of Otley Parish from 1837-1866, married Mr. Charles Garnett, a member of the Wharfeside Paper Mills family, but was left a widow after a short period of married life. In 1877, she helped to found the Mission which ministered to the needs, spiritual and temporal, of the navvy communities employed up and down the country in the construction of public works, such as the reservoirs at Swinsty, Fewston and Lindley.

After her death, a memorial tablet of Carrara and Irish marble, with the Navvy Mission badge carved at the top, was placed to her memory in Ripon Cathedral.

Navvy's friend, Mrs. Garnett

"Sings" at Whitsuntide

Church scholars in Manor Square, Whitsuntide 1879

One of the year's events in the Otley of the past most eagerly looked forward to was the annual "walk round and sing" of the Sunday School scholars on Whit Monday. In my young days, children only got new outfits once a year — a new suit for the boys, and a dress and hat for the girls — and this was at Whitsuntide, when they paraded the town to show off their new attire.

Scholars of the Church of England congregated in Manor Square to sing the hymns chosen for the occasion, and led by the Guiseley Brass Band; whilst those of the Sunday School Union, composed of the combined Nonconformist communities, used the Market Place, with the Otley Band in attendance. Afterwards came the march through the crowded streets, headed by the Bands, to the various Sunday Schools for dispersal, where a paper bag holding two large succulent buns, containing plenty of currents and raisins, together with an orange, was given to each child.

In the evening, sports and games were indulged in; the Nonconformists in Westbourne Park, and the Anglicans in the Cricket Field, where the Band in the latter played selections and also led the dancing. With the increase in traffic, the "walks" had eventually to be discontinued as being dangerous. The "sings" also were relegated to school yards, but these did not have the same appeal and gradually died out.

Non-conformist scholars in Market Square Whitsuntide, 1894

The Village Blacksmith

A building in Bridge Street that is now the surgery of a partnership of doctors, was formerly the blacksmith's shop, where the farmers of the surrounding countryside had their horses shod for many years. Outside the premises was an old stone watering trough which is now preserved in a yard at the rear.

The last working blacksmith there, who also owned the property, was Mr. Harry Hunt.

Many years ago, at this smithy, Tilly Whitley worked — a typical "village blacksmith", with brawny arms and massive head. He was an accomplished swimmer, and if anyone unfortunately fell into the river, Tilly was usually fetched to get them out. On one such occasion, after making a rescue, he said to the man he had got out of the water, "Tha owt ta gi'e me a sovereign for saving thi' life". "Nay," said the rescued, "Ah would rather have gi'en thee a sovereign to let me stop." Tilly was once presented with a gold watch and purse of money for saving life.

Old Smithy in Bridge Street 1887

120

The Manufacture of Tobacco

One of the few remaining family businesses in Otley is that of Messrs. Barbers, the Tobacconists, whose shop is in Kirkgate. Established in the last century by Mr. Joseph Barber, grandfather of the present proprietor — Jack — the premises are the third to be used as a retail shop, and they have all been in Kirkgate. The original factory and shop were, in my early days, on the East side of Kirkgate. Messrs. Woolworths' store now stands on this site. The retail shop faced on to the main road, and the factory, where the tobacco leaf was processed, was at the rear of the building; access was reached from a passage at the side, which ran from Kirkgate to New Market, known as "Barber's Yard". In former days it was called "Bullock Fold".

Quite a large wholesale business, in addition to the retail trade, was done by Mr. Barber, and a number of people were employed, mostly female. Mr. Joseph Barber also had his own tobacco plantation in Kentucky, U.S.A., which he often visited. In the year 1897, on behalf of himself and the Keighley and Bradford tobacco manufacturers, he imported over 100 hogsheads of the finest leaf tobacco ever to be made to this country. A special train of twenty-four wagons brought the consignment from Liverpool to the bonding warehouses at Bradford.

About the middle of 1800, Otley seems to have been the centre of the tobacco business, for Mr. Christopher Jackson, the proprietor of the grocery and provision business carried on at the "Old Corner Shop", was also a supplier of tobacco and snuff. I have seen a license issued to him by the Leeds Excise Office in 1843, which empowered him to manufacture these commodities

Stemming tobacco leaf at Barber's tobacco factory

Joseph Barber on his plantation in Kentucky U.S.A.

in Otley, for which a fee of ten guineas was charged. The business must have prospered for, in 1850, Mr. Jackson built, on the site of the "Grey Horse" Inn in Kirkgate, a small factory for the manufacture of the fragrant (or noxious, whichever way one thinks) weed. This building was at the rear of the present Yorkshire Bank, and was reached by a wide passage from Kirkgate.

Over the years since tobacco ceased to be manufactured there, these premises have been used in turn as a concert hall, working man's club, Salvation Army Citadel and a warehouse, before being pulled down in order to rebuild and extend the Yorkshire Bank premises adjoining.

First District Nurse

The first District Nurse in Otley was named Miss Nesbitt. The Nurses Home was then in Westgate, near Guycroft, and was opened in 1897 to commemorate Queen Victoria's Jubilee. It was given a public send-off at a big gathering of invited guests in the Recreation Hall, the host and hostess being the Chairman of Otley Urban District Council, Mr. W. H. Barker, and Mrs. Barker. It was intended to eventually inaugurate a cottage hospital scheme, and although this never materialized, a larger Nurses Home was built in Farnley Lane. This is now no longer in use since Social Security came into force, and a hospital was established in the district. In the few months between her appointment and the opening of the Nurses' Home in Westgate, Nurse Nesbitt had 106 patients, and paid 3,340 visits.

Otley's first District Nurse

Early Fire Engines

The Otley Local Board of Health, formed in 1864, and succeeded by the Urban District Council in 1894, had two manual fire engines presented to it. The first was given in 1864, by Mr. David Chippindale, an Otley plumber, who built and lived in Cambridge Cottage, and the other by Mrs. Emma Dawson, of Weston Hall, in 1875. She also provided the firemen — all local men — with tunics, belts and axes at her own expense.

Otley's First Fire Engine

Fire engine presented by Mrs. Emma Dawson

Miscellaneous Photographs

Demolition of the Black Horse in September 1900

Bondgate in 1890

Top of Boroughgate, showing the old George Inn

Milk delivery by Ben Cowburn

Market Square, on the right can be seen scales for the weighing of wool.

Wm. Walker's shop in Kirkgate, decorated for the Coronation of King Edward in 1902

Postmen outside the Post Office when it was in Boroughgate

Kirkgate in 1883 after a snowstorm

Queen Victoria's Golden Jubilee bonfire on Chevin

Laying sewer pipes across the river, about 1899

*The old leper houses in Cross Green, sketched by W.
Longfield*

*Old alms houses, also in Cross Green, sketched by W.
Longfield*

Supt. Strain and members of Otley Police team, first winners of the Wharfedale Ambulance Trophy

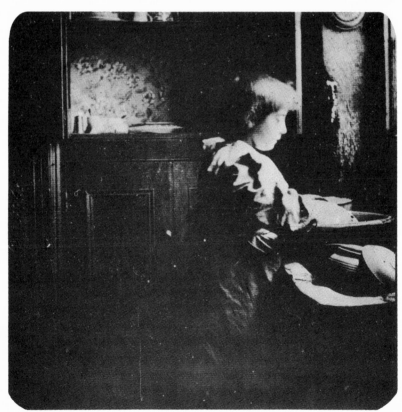

The kitchen sink in 1888

First trackless tram between Guiseley and Otley, Sept. 8th, 1915

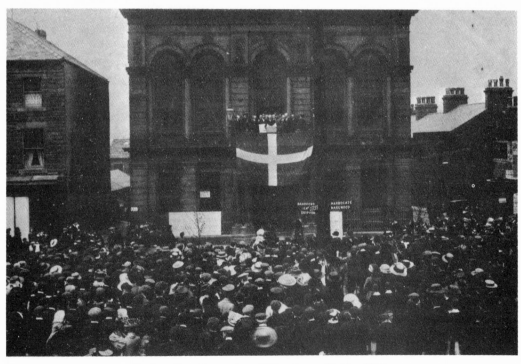

Proclamation of accession of King George V, May 1910

Past Schoolmasters

One of Otley's early schoolmasters, named Mr. Tunnicliffe, was reputed in his day to be one of the finest pen-men in England, and a specimen of his work — "The Lord's Prayer" — considered to be a work of art. Another member of the profession, Mr. Sharphouse, conducted a boys' school in the old Quaker Meeting House in Cross. Green, on the site of which now stand the premises of the Christian (formerly the Plymouth) Brethren. This man, very eccentric and also intensely religious, was in the habit of writing on a blackboard at the beginning of each school year, for the benefit of new scholars, the words: "A liar I do detest." He was firmly convinced of the second coming of Jesus Christ on earth: "and boys", he would shout, "I shall be there to see Him." Mr. Sharphouse resided in a little thatched cottage adjoining the Meeting House.

Mr. Sharphouse

Specimen of Mr. Tunnicliffe's work

An Eminent Cleric

An Otley lad, born in a cottage in Cross Green in 1873, became the Venerable Archdeacon Dawson, of Milwauki, Winsconsin, U.S.A. The son of James and Margaret Dawson, the family lived in Chevin Side, near the Old Vicarage, and at West Chevin End, by the Chevin Inn, before removing to Bradford. It was from the latter town that young William emigrated alone to the United States, at the age of 19, to work his way through college and finally enter the Christian ministry. Archdeacon Dawson's grandparents on his mother's side, were named Ingham, and resided at one time at the old Weigh House in Boroughgate, on the site of which now stands the Unionist Club.

During the 1939-46 War, one of his sons, Lt. Col. Gordon E. Dawson of the 10th Mountain Division, United States Army, which was trained in the High Rocky Mountains, saw service in Italy in 1944, where the Unit accomplished what the German Army considered to be an impossible feat. This was to cross the River Po and climb the Apennine Mountains to go into action.

Archdeacon Dawson was proud of being born in Otley, and on the one or two visits he paid to the town in his later years, was deluged with a sense of its history and tradition. The following sonnet he wrote expresses the depth of his feelings :—

"Otley in Wharfedale, illustrious name,
    That turns my heart to lullabys of praise
For thee that mothered me through childhood days;
    I was part of thee — from thee I came.
Inspired by thy beauty and thy fame,
    After the passing years, this fondness stays
For thy quaint streets, old shops, thy people's ways —
    The soul of love's first love remains the same.
I dream of Jenny's Hill above the town,
    Thy Norman Church, Kirkgate and Burras Lane,
East Chevin where I wandered up and down —
    The Otley Bridge — Wharfe swollen with the rain;
This heritage, I wear it as a crown,
    And dance around thy Maypole once again."

What a fitting conclusion these lines make to my memories of "THIS LITTLE TOWN OF OTLEY".